This I Believe

This I Believe®

THE PERSONAL PHILOSOPHIES
OF REMARKABLE
MEN AND WOMEN

EDITED BY
Jay Allison AND Dan Gediman
WITH John Gregory AND Viki Merrick

EDITORIAL TEAM (1950S SERIES)
Gladys Chang Hardy, Reny Hill,
Donald J. Merwin, Edward P. Morgan,
Edward R. Murrow, Raymond Swing,
Ward Wheelock

EDITORIAL TEAM (CONTEMPORARY SERIES)
Bruce Auster, Emily Botein,
Susan Feeney, Ellen Silva

A HOLT PAPERBACK
HENRY HOLT AND COMPANY • NEW YORK

Holt Paperbacks
Henry Holt and Company, LLC
Publishers since 1866
175 Fifth Avenue
New York, New York 10010
www.henryholt.com

A Holt Paperback® and ®® are registered trademarks of Henry Holt and Company, LLC.

Copyright © 2007 by This I Believe, Inc.
All rights reserved.

NPR, National Public Radio, All Things Considered, Morning Edition, and their logos are registered and unregistered service marks of National Public Radio, Inc.

Distributed in Canada by H. B. Fenn and Company Ltd.

Library of Congress Cataloging-in-Publication Data

This I believe: the personal philosophies of remarkable men and women / edited by Jay Allison and Dan Gediman ; with John Gregory and Viki Merrick.
    p. cm.
ISBN-13: 978-0-8050-8658-4
ISBN-10: 0-8050-8658-7
    1. Belief and doubt. 2. Conduct of life. 3. Life. 4. Celebrities. I. Allison, Jay. II. Gediman, Dan. III. Gregory, John. IV. Merrick, Viki.

BD215.T46 2006
170'.44—dc22   2006043522

Henry Holt books are available for special promotions and premiums.
For details contact: Director, Special Markets.

Originally published in hardcover in 2006 by Henry Holt and Company

First Holt Paperbacks Edition 2007

Designed by Meryl Sussman Levavi
Printed in the United States of America
10 9 8 7 6 5 4 3 2 1

To Margot Trevor Wheelock, who was responsible for This I Believe

Contents

Foreword — xvii
STUDS TERKEL

Introduction — 1
JAY ALLISON

Be Cool to the Pizza Dude — 7
SARAH ADAMS

Leaving Identity Issues to Other Folks — 10
PHYLLIS ALLEN

In Giving I Connect with Others — 13
ISABEL ALLENDE

Remembering All the Boys — 16
ELVIA BAUTISTA

The Mountain Disappears — 19
LEONARD BERNSTEIN

How Is It Possible to Believe in God? — 22
WILLIAM F. BUCKLEY, JR.

The Fellowship of the World — 25
NIVEN BUSCH

Contents

There Is No Job More Important than Parenting — 28
　BENJAMIN CARSON

A Journey toward Acceptance and Love — 31
　GREG CHAPMAN

A Shared Moment of Trust — 34
　WARREN CHRISTOPHER

The Hardest Work You Will Ever Do — 37
　MARY COOK

Good Can Be as Communicable as Evil — 40
　NORMAN CORWIN

A Daily Walk Just to Listen — 43
　SUSAN COSIO

The Elusive Yet Holy Core — 46
　KATHY DAHLEN

My Father's Evening Star — 49
　WILLIAM O. DOUGLAS

An Honest Doubter — 52
Have I Learned Anything Important Since I Was Sixteen? — 55
　ELIZABETH DEUTSCH EARLE

An Ideal of Service to Our Fellow Man — 58
　ALBERT EINSTEIN

The Power and Mystery of Naming Things — 62
　EVE ENSLER

Contents

A Goal of Service to Humankind   65
    ANTHONY FAUCI

The God Who Embraced Me   68
    JOHN W. FOUNTAIN

Unleashing the Power of Creativity   71
    BILL GATES

The People Who Love You When No One Else Will   75
    CECILE GILMER

The Willingness to Work for Solutions   78
    NEWT GINGRICH

The Connection between Strangers   81
    MILES GOODWIN

An Athlete of God   84
    MARTHA GRAHAM

Seeing in Beautiful, Precise Pictures   87
    TEMPLE GRANDIN

Disrupting My Comfort Zone   90
    BRIAN GRAZER

Science Nourishes the Mind and the Soul   93
    BRIAN GREENE

In Praise of the "Wobblies"   97
    TED GUP

Contents

The Power of Presence   100
   DEBBIE HALL

A Grown-Up Barbie   103
   JANE HAMILL

Happy Talk   106
   OSCAR HAMMERSTEIN II

Natural Links in a Long Chain of Being   109
   VICTOR HANSON

Talking with the Sun   112
   JOY HARJO

A Morning Prayer in a Little Church   115
   HELEN HAYES

Our Noble, Essential Decency   119
   ROBERT A. HEINLEIN

A New Birth of Freedom   123
   MAXIMILIAN HODDER

The Benefits of Restlessness and Jagged Edges   126
   KAY REDFIELD JAMISON

There Is No God   129
   PENN JILLETTE

A Duty to Heal   132
   PIUS KAMAU

Contents

Living Life with "Grace and Elegant Treeness"   135
   RUTH KAMPS

The Light of a Brighter Day   138
   HELEN KELLER

The Bright Lights of Freedom   141
   HAROLD HONGJU KOH

The Power of Love to Transform and Heal   144
   JACKIE LANTRY

The Power of Mysteries   147
   ALAN LIGHTMAN

Life Grows in the Soil of Time   150
   THOMAS MANN

Why I Close My Restaurant   153
   GEORGE MARDIKIAN

The Virtues of the Quiet Hero   156
   JOHN MCCAIN

The Joy and Enthusiasm of Reading   159
   RICK MOODY

There Is Such a Thing as Truth   162
   ERROL MORRIS

The Rule of Law   165
   MICHAEL MULLANE

Contents

Getting Angry Can Be a Good Thing — 168
    CECILIA MUÑOZ

Mysterious Connections That Link Us Together — 171
    AZAR NAFISI

The Making of Poems — 175
    GREGORY ORR

We Are Each Other's Business — 178
    EBOO PATEL

The 50-Percent Theory of Life — 181
    STEVE PORTER

The America I Believe In — 184
    COLIN POWELL

The Real Consequences of Justice — 188
    FREDERIC REAMER

There Is More to Life than My Life — 191
    JAMAICA RITCHER

Tomorrow Will Be a Better Day — 194
    JOSH RITTENBERG

Free Minds and Hearts at Work — 197
    JACKIE ROBINSON

Growth That Starts from Thinking — 201
    ELEANOR ROOSEVELT

The Artistry in Hidden Talents MEL RUSNOV	204
My Fellow Worms CARL SANDBURG	207
When Children Are Wanted MARGARET SANGER	210
Jazz Is the Sound of God Laughing COLLEEN SHADDOX	214
There Is No Such Thing as Too Much Barbecue JASON SHEEHAN	217
The People Have Spoken MARK SHIELDS	220
Everything Potent Is Dangerous WALLACE STEGNER	224
A Balance between Nature and Nurture GLORIA STEINEM	228
Life, Liberty, and the Pursuit of Happiness ANDREW SULLIVAN	232
Always Go to the Funeral DEIRDRE SULLIVAN	235
Finding Prosperity by Feeding Monkeys HAROLD TAW	238

I Agree with a Pagan	241
ARNOLD TOYNBEE	
Testing the Limits of What I Know and Feel	244
JOHN UPDIKE	
How Do You Believe in a Mystery?	247
LOUDON WAINWRIGHT III	
Creative Solutions to Life's Challenges	250
FRANK X WALKER	
Goodness Doesn't Just Happen	253
REBECCA WEST	
When Ordinary People Achieve Extraordinary Things	257
JODY WILLIAMS	
Afterword: The History of This I Believe*: The Power of an Idea*	260
DAN GEDIMAN	
APPENDIX A: *Introduction to the 1950s* This I Believe *Radio Series*	269
EDWARD R. MURROW	
APPENDIX B: *How to Write Your Own* This I Believe *Essay*	272
APPENDIX C: *How to Use* This I Believe *in Your Community*	274
Acknowledgments	276
Reader's Guide	285

Foreword

STUDS TERKEL

"AT A TIME WHEN THE TIDE RUNS toward a sure conformity, when dissent is often confused with subversion, when a man's belief may be subject to investigation as well as his actions..."

It has the ring of a 2006 mayday call of distress, yet it was written in 1952. Ed Murrow, introducing an assemblage of voices in the volume *This I Believe*, sounded a claxon.

It is an old story yet ever-contemporary. In 1791, Tom Paine, the most eloquent visionary of the American Revolution, sounded off:

> Freedom has been hunted around the globe; reason was considered as rebellion; and the slavery of fear made man afraid to think. But such is the irresistible nature of truth is that all it asks, and all it wants, is the liberty of appearing . . . In such a situation, man becomes what he ought to be. He sees his species not with the inhuman idea of a natural enemy, but as kindred . . .

It is the pursuit of this truth that appears to be the common tenor of all the voices you hear in this new volume.

We need not dwell on the old question: What is truth? What you see with your own eyes may differ from the received official truth. So old Pilate had only one decision to make: find the man guilty or he, the judge, will be sent back to the boondocks. Pilate did what any well-behaved hack would do. Though he had his hands scrubbed and rub-a-dub-dubbed with Ivory soap, 99.44% pure, he could not erase the awful truth of the dirt on his hands. Though Pilate's wife pleaded for a show of mercy, he made an objective decision.

In our time, James Cameron, the nonpareil of British journalism, dealt with the matter in his own way. "I cannot remember how often I've been challenged for disregarding the fundamental tenet of honest journalism, which is objectivity."

His bearing witness in North Vietnam during that war convinced him, despite all official Washington arguments to the contrary, that North Vietnam was inhabited by human beings. He was condemned for being non-objective and having a point of view. Cameron confesses, "I may not have always been satisfactorily balanced; I always tended to argue that objectivity was of less importance than the truth."

Errol Morris, film documentarian, who appears in this book, shares the obstinancy of Cameron: "Truth is not relative.... It may be elusive or hidden. People may wish to disregard it. But there is such a thing as truth." What really possesses Morris is the pursuit of the truth: "Trying to figure out what has really happened, trying to figure out how things really are."

The chase is what it's all about. The quarry is, as always, the truth.

On a small patch of Sag Harbor dirt is a simple stone easily passed by. Nelson Algren is buried there and his epitaph is simple: "The journey is all."

Andrew Sullivan, editor of *The New Republic*, who appears in this volume, has a similar vision. He and Algren may have differed considerably in their political views, yet here, as to fundamental belief, they were as one. "I believe in the pursuit of happiness. Not its attainment, nor its final definition, but its pursuit."

I'd be remiss with no mention of Helen Keller, whose vision we saw and whose voice we heard fifty years ago, a deaf, dumb, and blind child. It was her sense of wonder and her pursuit of truth which she saw much more clearly than sighted people, and heard much more clearly than hearing folk. They were voices in need throughout the world she heard so vividly. Above all it was her faith that the human being was better than his/her behavior.

What I believe is a compote of these ingredients. Yes I do have a point of view which I express much too frequently, I suspect. And yet there's always that uncertainty. In all my adventures among hundreds of Americans I have discovered that the rule of thumb does not work. I've been astonished too often by those I've visited: ordinary Americans, who at times, are extraordinary in their insights and dreams.

I find the labels "liberal" and "conservative" of little meaning. Our language has become perverted along with the thoughts of many of us.

"Liberal" according to any dictionary is defined as the freedom to speak out, no matter what the official word may be, and the right to defend all others who speak out whether or not they agree with you. "Conservative" is the word I've always associated with conserving our environment from pollution, ensuring that our water is potable and our grass green. So I declare myself a radical conservative. Radical, as in getting to the root of things. Pasteur was a radical. Semmelweiss was a radical. "Wash your hands," he declared to doctors and nurses. He may have wound up in a nuthouse, but he pursued the truth, found it, and saved untold millions of lives. I am a conservative in that I'm out to conserve the blue of the sky, the freshness of the air of which we have less and less, the First Amendment of the Bill of Rights, and whatever semblance of sanity we may have left. As for faith, I've always called myself an agnostic. Were Ambrose Bierce alive today, he would no doubt have added to his *Devil's Dictionary:* "An agnostic is a cowardly atheist." Perhaps. But perhaps I do believe there is a God deposited in each of us ever since the Big Bang.

I secretly envy those who believe in the hereafter and with it the idea that they may once again meet dear ones. They cannot prove beyond a reasonable doubt that there is such a place. Neither can I disprove it. I cannot find the bookmaker willing to take my bet on it. How will one who guesses right be able to collect his winnings? So speaking on behalf of the bookies of the world, all bets are off.

Maybe the poet Keats was right after all in the "Ode on a Grecian Urn." He envied the fortunate youth who is forever chasing his love, never quite catching her. The pursuit is all.

And yet there is something which I believe with no uncertainty. There is something we can do while we're alive and breathing on this planet. It is to become an activist in this pursuit of a world in which it would be easier for people to behave decently. (I am paraphrasing Dorothy Day, who founded the Catholic Worker Movement.)

Being an activist is self-explanatory: you act; you take part in something outside yourself. You join with others, who may astonish you in thinking precisely as you do on the subjects, say, of war, civil liberties, human rights.

My belief came into being during the most traumatic moment in American history, the Great Depression of the 1930s. I remember seeing pots and pans and bedsteads and mattresses on the sidewalks. A family had just been evicted and there was an individual cry of despair, multiplied by millions. But that community had a number of people on that very block, electricians and plumbers and carpenters, who appeared that very evening, and moved the household goods back into the flat where they had been. They turned on the gas, they fixed the plumbing. It was a community in action accomplishing something.

Albert Einstein once observed that westerners have a feeling the individual loses his freedom if he joins, say, a union or any group. Precisely the opposite is the case. Once you join others, even though at first your mission fails, you become a different person, a much stronger one. You feel that you really count, you discover your strength as an individual because you have along the way discovered others share in what you believe, you are not alone; and thus a community is formed. I am paraphrasing Einstein. I love to do that; nobody dares contradict me.

So, my credo consists of the pursuit *and the act*. One without the other is self-indulgence. This I believe.

This I Believe

Introduction

Jay Allison

This I Believe OFFERS A SIMPLE, IF DIFFICULT INVITATION: Write a few hundred words expressing the core principles that guide your life—your personal credo.

We issue that invitation to politicians, nurses, artists, construction workers, athletes, parents, students, the famous, and the unknown, everyone. All the essayists in this book accepted the invitation.

There is risk in what they did. They wrote of their most closely held convictions and then spoke them on the radio to an audience of millions in a media climate that tends toward sound bites, potshots, and spin. To make such an earnest, exposed statement is itself an act of bravery. We who read the dozens of essays that arrive each morning in our e-mail recognize this act. It touches us, and it is not too much to say that we approach our work with a sense of honor.

All the editors of this series know how difficult it is to write one of these essays, because we have tried it. The editors of the original series in the 1950s did, too. Like most of the thousands we've received, these essays won't be on the radio and, in most cases, won't be read by anyone other than the writer. But we believe the exercise is important. The attempt alone has value.

At its heart, this book is an invitation to make the attempt yourself.

This I Believe was first broadcast in 1951, with Edward R. Murrow hosting. A team of editors worked on the project for five years, making the series a daily radio staple and eventually a publishing phenomenon.

Fifty years after the original series ended, we felt the time was right to bring it back. As in the 1950s, matters of belief divide our country and the world. We find ourselves in conflict over moral standards, patriotism, family, and issues of race and faith. Yet amid the most pervasive information delivery systems in history, there is little place for the encouragement of quiet listening to the beliefs of others without rebuttal or criticism.

More and more, news output is based not so much on the events of the day but those of the moment. An hour old is old. When does the value of immediacy wear out? When we know what has happened in the last second? The last millisecond? *This I Believe* heads in the other direction. It is interested not in what can be learned in a moment but over a lifetime. When *This I Believe* essays appear in the midst of the NPR news programs *All Things Considered* and *Morning Edition*, time changes a little. The din of the daily is left behind, and the moment is noted not for its clamor but its calm.

In our revival of *This I Believe*, we have been guided by the original team. We make the same requests of essayists that they did: Frame your beliefs in positive terms. Refrain from dwelling on what you do not believe. Avoid restatement of doctrine. Focus on the personal, the "I" of the title, not the subtly sermonizing "We." While you may hold many beliefs, write mainly of one. Aim for truth without accusation, patriotism without political cant, and faith beyond religious dogma.

We have found that some writers do best to tell a story, perhaps of a moment a belief was forged, or tested, or confirmed. Others peel the onion of what they were taught to believe, what they think they should believe, and even what they always believed they *would* believe.

In this volume you will find essays from fifty years ago intermingled with essays of today. The themes are not very different. People still search for meaning, want to help others, try to overcome fear, wonder at death and birth. While we may now be more casual in style, this exercise often summons a formal declaration, a statement considered enough to stand up for.

A word on process. One distinction between our series and the 1950s is our public call for essays. We accept submissions over the Internet via our Web site (www.thisibelieve.org). As of this writing (spring 2007), more than 22,000 essays have been read by our reviewing team in Woods Hole, Massachusetts. We flag essays that stand out for their expressiveness, their perspective, or simply because we remember them. All essayists, those we invite to write for our series and also those whose essays are chosen from Internet submissions, are edited for radio—sometimes a little, sometimes a lot—until everyone is content. Writers usually record in studios near where they live, while I coach their readings over the phone. Finally, our photographer visits them to take their portraits.

In reading the submissions, we have noticed trends. Many offer testimony to such principles as the Golden Rule, living in the moment, the importance of love and giving. Others write of family, god, and country. Deep lessons are learned in proximity to illness and death, when the value of life is felt more keenly; Alzheimer's, for example, often occasions an examination of the fundamental nature of personality and belief. It may also be worth noting some common rhetorical pitfalls: self-righteousness, prescribing for others, advertisements for self, cliché, and disguised attack.

Most essayists make earnest attempts to determine what they believe for themselves. In our online submission form, we have a space for reflections on the process. Writers express gratitude for the opportunity, the nudge, to take on the challenge. They generally don't find it easy. One said it was like packing for a long trip using an overnight bag. Some tell of sharing their essays with others, "broadcasting" them in their own circles. *This I Believe* essays have been read at weddings and funerals, given and asked for on birthdays. Colleges and schools around the country have undertaken the project; one school in Vermont packed the local public library for a night of essay readings. Once they assign students the task of writing an essay, teachers report they feel obligated to complete one, too. For those who may be interested, the appendices of this book contain a history of the series, guidelines for essayists, and resources for writers, teachers, places of worship, and community groups. An online archive of every submitted essay can be found at our Web site.

* * *

Beliefs are choices. No one has authority over your personal beliefs. Your beliefs are in jeopardy only when you don't know what they are.

Understanding your own beliefs, and those of others, comes through focused thought and discussion. Most public dialogue is now propelled by media outlets owned by a dwindling number of multinational corporations. A healthy democracy needs ways to bypass gatekeepers so we can communicate with one another directly, and perhaps even find common ground. *This I Believe* is an exercise in philosophical self-examination in a public context. It rises from the grass roots, where people can begin to listen to each other, one at a time.

My own *This I Believe* essay begins, "I believe in listening . . ." This is no surprise, coming from one who works in radio, and public radio at that. At the station in my hometown, it's our motto, and the first word ever spoken on the air when we signed on. *Listen.* If there is a testament to a belief in listening, it will be found in these essays.

Take a moment, then, to consider the beliefs that guide the lives of others, beliefs that may confirm your own, or challenge them, or even open your mind to something new.

When you are done, think about this: What would *you* say?

Be Cool to the Pizza Dude

SARAH ADAMS

IF I HAVE ONE OPERATING PHILOSOPHY ABOUT LIFE, it is this: "Be cool to the pizza delivery dude; it's good luck." Four principles guide the pizza dude philosophy.

Principle 1: Coolness to the pizza delivery dude is a practice in humility and forgiveness. I let him cut me off in traffic, let him safely hit the exit ramp from the left lane, let him forget to use his blinker without extending any of my digits out the window or toward my horn because there should be one moment in my harried life when a car may encroach or cut off or pass and I let it go. Sometimes when I have become so certain of my ownership of my lane, daring anyone to challenge me, the pizza dude speeds by in his rusted Chevette. His pizza light atop his car glowing like a beacon reminds me to check myself as I flow through the world. After all, the dude is delivering pizza to young and old, families and singletons, gays and straights, blacks, whites, and browns, rich and poor, and vegetarians and meat lovers alike. As he journeys, I give safe passage, practice restraint, show courtesy, and contain my anger.

Principle 2: Coolness to the pizza delivery dude is a practice in empathy. Let's face it: We've all taken jobs just to have a job because some money is better than none. I've held an assortment of these jobs and was grateful for the paycheck that meant I didn't have to share my Cheerios with my cats. In the big pizza wheel of life, sometimes you're the hot bubbly cheese and sometimes you're the burnt crust. It's good to remember the fickle spinning of that wheel.

Principle 3: Coolness to the pizza delivery dude is a practice in honor, and it reminds me to honor honest work. Let me tell you something about these dudes: They never took over a company and, as CEO, artificially inflated the value of the stock and cashed out their own shares, bringing the company to the brink of bankruptcy, resulting in twenty thousand people losing their jobs while the CEO builds a home the size of a luxury hotel. Rather, the dudes sleep the sleep of the just.

Principle 4: Coolness to the pizza delivery dude is a practice in equality. My measurement as a human being, my worth, is the pride I take in performing my job—any job—and the respect with which I treat others. I am the equal of the world not because of the car I drive, the size of the TV I own, the weight I can bench-press, or the calculus equations I can solve. I am the equal to all I meet because of the kindness in my heart. And it all starts here—with the pizza delivery dude.

Tip him well, friends and brethren, for that which you bestow freely and willingly will bring you all the happy luck that a grateful universe knows how to return.

Sarah Adams has held many jobs in her life, including telemarketer, factory worker, hotel clerk, and flower shop cashier, but she has never delivered pizzas. Raised in Wisconsin, Adams is now an English professor at Olympic College in Washington.

Leaving Identity Issues to Other Folks

PHYLLIS ALLEN

STANDING IN THE RAIN WAITING TO GO up the steps to the balcony of the Grand Theater, I gripped Mama's hand and watched the little blond kids enter the lobby downstairs. It was the fifties, I was "colored," and this is what I believed: My place was in the balcony of the downtown theater, the back of the bus, and the back steps of the White Dove Barbecue Emporium. When I asked Mama why this was so, she smiled and said, "Baby, people do what they do. What you got to do is be the best that you can be."

We got our first television in the sixties, and it brought into my living room the German shepherds, snapping at a young girl's heels. It showed children just like me going to school passing through throngs of screaming, angry folks, chanting words I wasn't allowed to say. I could no longer be "colored." We were Negroes now, marching in the streets for our freedom—at least, that's what the preacher said. I believed that even though I was scared, I had to be brave and stand up for my rights.

In the seventies: Beat-up jeans, hair like a nappy halo, and my clenched fist raised, I stood on the downtown street shouting. Angry young black men in sleek black leather jackets and berets had sent out a call from the distant shores of Oakland, California. No more nonviolence or standing on the front lines quietly while we were being beaten. Simple courtesies like "please" and "thank you" were over. It was official; Huey, H. Rap, and Eldridge said so. I believed in being black and angry.

By the eighties, fertility gods lined the walls and crammed the display cases of all my friends' houses. People who'd never been closer to Africa than a *Tarzan* movie were speaking broken Swahili. The eighties made us hyphenated: "African-American." Swaddled in elaborately woven costumes of flowing design, bright colors, and rich gold, I was a pseudo-African, who'd never seen Africa. "It's your heritage," is what everybody said. Now, I believed in the elusive promise of the Motherland.

In the nineties, I was a woman whose skin happened to be brown, chasing the American dream. Everybody said that the dream culminated in stuff. I believed in spending days shopping. Debt? I didn't care about no stinkin' debt. It was the nineties. My 401(k) was in the mid-six figures, and I believed in American Express. Then came the crash, and American Express didn't believe in me nearly as much as I believed in it.

Now, it's a brand-new millennium, and the bling-bling, video generation ain't about me. Everything changed when I turned fifty. Along with the wrinkles, softened muscles, and weak eyesight came the confidence that allows me to stick to a very small list of beliefs. I'll leave those identity issues to other folks. I believe that I'm free to be whoever I choose to be. I believe in being a good friend, lover, and parent so that I can have good friends, lovers, and children. I believe in being a woman—the best that I can be, like my mama said.

Phyllis Allen *has sold* Yellow Pages *advertising for fifteen years. She spends about half her working hours in her car covering territory around Dallas and Fort Worth, Texas. She composed her essay in her car and practiced reading it aloud in the phone company's utility closet. When she retires, she hopes to pursue her first passion, writing.*

In Giving I Connect with Others

Isabel Allende

I HAVE LIVED WITH PASSION AND IN A HURRY, trying to accomplish too many things. I never had time to think about my beliefs until my twenty-eight-year-old daughter Paula fell ill. She was in a coma for a year, and I took care of her at home until she died in my arms in December of 1992.

During that year of agony and the following year of my grieving, everything stopped for me. There was nothing to do—just cry and remember. However, that year also gave me an opportunity to reflect upon my journey and the principles that hold me together. I discovered that there is consistency in my beliefs, my writing, and the way I lead my life. I have not changed; I am still the same girl I was fifty years ago, and the same young woman I was in the seventies. I still lust for life, I am still ferociously independent, I still crave justice, and I fall madly in love easily.

Paralyzed and silent in her bed, my daughter Paula taught me a lesson that is now my mantra: You only have what you give. It's by spending yourself that you become rich.

Paula led a life of service. She worked as a volunteer helping women and children, eight hours a day, six days a week. She never had any money, but she needed very little. When she died she had nothing and she needed nothing. During her illness I had to let go of everything: her laughter, her voice, her grace, her beauty, her company, and, finally, her spirit. When she died I thought I had lost everything. But then I realized I still had the love I had given her. I don't even know if she was able to receive that love. She could not respond in any way, her eyes were somber pools that reflected no light. But I was full of love, and that love keeps growing and multiplying and giving fruit.

The pain of losing my child was a cleansing experience. I had to throw overboard all excess baggage and keep only what is essential. Because of Paula, I don't cling to anything anymore. Now I like to give much more than to receive. I am happier when I love than when I am loved. I adore my husband, my son, my grandchildren, my mother, my dog, and frankly I don't know if they even like me. But who cares? Loving them is my joy.

Give, give, give—what is the point of having experience, knowledge, or talent if I don't give it away? Of having stories if I don't tell them to others? Of having wealth if I don't share it? I don't intend to be cremated with any of it! It is in giving that I connect with others, with the world, and with the divine.

It is in giving that I feel the spirit of my daughter inside me, like a soft presence.

Novelist ISABEL ALLENDE *was born in Peru and raised in Chile. When her uncle, Chilean president Salvador Allende, was assassinated in 1973, she fled with her husband and children to Venezuela. Allende has written more than a dozen novels, including* The House of the Spirits *and a memoir,* My Invented Country.

Remembering All the Boys

Elvia Bautista

I BELIEVE THAT EVERYONE DESERVES flowers on their grave.

When I go to the cemetery to visit my brother, it makes me sad to see graves—just the cold stones—and no flowers on them.

They look lonely, like nobody loves them. I believe this is the worst thing in the world—that loneliness. No one to visit you and brush off the dust from your name and cover you with color. A grave without any flowers looks like the person has been forgotten. And then what was the point of even living—to be forgotten?

Almost every day my brother's grave has something new

on it: flowers from me, or candles from the Dollar Store, or an image of the Virgin Maria, or shot glasses. There's even some little Homies, these little toys that look like gangsters.

Once my brother's homies even put a bunch of marijuana on there for him—I think my mother took it away. I think she also took away the blue rag someone put there for him one day.

Sometimes, when I bring flowers, I fix the flowers on the graves around my brother's grave. Some of the headstones have birthdates near my brother's; they are young, too. But many of them, if they have any little toys or things on them, those are red.

All around my brother are boys who grew up to like red, making them the enemies of my brother. My brother was sixteen when he was shot by someone who liked red, who killed him because he liked blue. And when I go to the cemetery, I put flowers on the graves of the boys who liked red, too.

Sometimes I go to the cemetery with one of my best friends, who had a crush on a boy who liked red who was killed at eighteen by someone who liked blue. And we will go together and bring a big bunch of flowers, enough for both of these boys whose families are actually even from the same state in Mexico.

There is no one but me and a few of my friends who go

to both graves. Some people think it's a bad idea. Some people think it's heroic.

I think they're both being silly. I don't go to try to disrespect some special rules or stop any kind of war. I go because I believe that no matter where you came from or what you believed in, when you die, you want flowers on your grave and people who visit you and remember you that way.

I'm not any kind of traitor or any kind of hero. I am the sister of Rogelio Bautista, and I say his name so you will hear it and be one more person who remembers him. I want everyone to remember all the boys, red and blue, in my cemetery. When we remember, we put flowers on their graves.

ELVIA BAUTISTA, *twenty-two, lives in Santa Rosa, California, where she works as a caregiver for the elderly and mentally handicapped. Bautista stayed after her brother's murder even though the rest of her family moved away. A high school dropout, Bautista now speaks to young people about the dangers of gang life.*

The Mountain Disappears

Leonard Bernstein,
as featured in the 1950s series

I BELIEVE IN PEOPLE. I feel, love, need, and respect people above all else, including the arts, natural scenery, organized piety, or nationalistic superstructures. One human figure on the slope of a mountain can make the whole mountain disappear for me. One person fighting for the truth can disqualify for me the platitudes of centuries. And one human being who meets with injustice can render invalid the entire system which has dispensed it.

I believe that man's noblest endowment is his capacity to change. Armed with reason, he can see two sides and choose: He can be divinely wrong. I believe in man's right to be wrong. Out of this right he has built, laboriously and lovingly, something we reverently call democracy. He has done it the hard way and continues to do it the hard way—by reason, by choosing, by error and rectification, by the difficult, slow method in which the dignity of A is acknowledged by B, without impairing the dignity of C. Man cannot have dignity without loving the dignity of his fellow.

I believe in the potential of people. I cannot rest passively with those who give up in the name of "human nature." Human nature is only animal nature if it is obliged to remain static. Without growth, without metamorphosis, there is no godhead. If we believe that man can never achieve a society without wars, then we are condemned to wars forever. This is the easy way. But the laborious, loving way, the way of dignity and divinity, presupposes a belief in people and in their capacity to change, grow, communicate, and love.

I believe in man's unconscious mind, the deep spring from which comes his power to communicate and to love. For me, all art is a combination of these powers; for if love is the way we have of communicating personally in the deepest way, then what art can do is to extend this communication, magnify it, and carry it to vastly greater numbers of people. Therefore art is valid for the warmth and love it carries within it, even if it be the lightest entertainment, or the bitterest satire, or the most shattering tragedy.

I believe that my country is the place where all these things I have been speaking of are happening in the most manifest way. America is at the beginning of her greatest period in history—a period of leadership in science, art, and human progress toward the democratic ideal. I believe that she is at a critical point in this moment and that she needs us to believe more strongly than ever before in her and in one another, in our ability to grow and change, in our mutual dignity, in our democratic method. We must encourage thought, free and creative. We must respect privacy. We must observe taste by not exploiting our sorrows, successes, or passions. We must learn to know ourselves better through art. We must rely more on the unconscious, inspirational side of man. We must not enslave ourselves to dogma. We must believe in the attainability of good. We must believe, without fear, in people.

Composer, conductor, pianist, and educator, LEONARD BERNSTEIN *was longtime music director of the New York Philharmonic, where he led the highly successful* Young People's Concerts *series. Bernstein forged a new relationship between classical and popular music with his compositions* West Side Story, On the Town, Candide, *and others.*

How Is It Possible to Believe in God?

William F. Buckley, Jr.

I'VE ALWAYS LIKED THE EXCHANGE FEATURING the excited young Darwinian at the end of the nineteenth century. He said grandly to the elderly scholar, "How is it possible to believe in God?" The imperishable answer was, "I find it easier to believe in God than to believe that *Hamlet* was deduced from the molecular structure of a mutton chop."

That rhetorical bullet has everything—wit and profundity. It has more than once reminded me that skepticism about life and nature is most often expressed by those who take it for granted that belief is an indulgence of the superstitious—

indeed their opiate, to quote a historical cosmologist most profoundly dead. Granted, that to look up at the stars comes close to compelling disbelief—how can such a chance arrangement be other than an elaboration—near infinite—of natural impulses? Yes, on the other hand, who is to say that the arrangement of the stars is more easily traceable to nature, than to nature's molder? What is the greater miracle: the raising of the dead man in Lazarus, or the mere existence of the man who died and the witnesses who swore to his revival?

The skeptics get away with fixing the odds against the believer, mostly by pointing to phenomena which are only explainable—you see?—by the belief that there was a cause for them, always deducible. But how can one deduce the cause of *Hamlet?* Or of *St. Matthew's Passion?* What is the cause of inspiration?

This I believe: that it is intellectually easier to credit a divine intelligence than to submit dumbly to felicitous congeries about nature. As a child, I was struck by the short story. It told of a man at a bar who boasted of his rootlessness, derisively dismissing the jingoistic patrons to his left and to his right. But later in the evening, one man speaks an animadversion on a little principality in the Balkans and is met with the clenched fist of the man without a country, who would not endure this insult to the place where he was born.

So I believe that it is as likely that there should be a man without a country, as a world without a creator.

WILLIAM F. BUCKLEY, JR., *founded* National Review *magazine in 1955 and was its editor for many years. As a conservative commentator, he was the host of the long-running public television program* Firing Line. *Buckley is also the author of the acclaimed series of Blackford Oakes spy novels.*

The Fellowship of the World

Niven Busch,
as featured in the 1950s series

When people utter an expression of their inner faith, the same words keep on cropping up: God, man, dignity, the future, the earth, forever, and so on. Usually such words have a meaning to me, only when my mind is very clear. When I am lying awake at night or, best of all out in the country on my ranch, perhaps going somewhere on a horse, then a wonderful sense of goodness and lightness comes into me, and I can think of life in the abstract. Then I can remember the old Spanish saying: "When I am on my horse, only God is taller than I."

Yet such times of wisdom are rare in my life and I think

in most people's. It is hard to separate one's thoughts from the pressure of the moment. Peace of mind is like the country, but active life itself is like a city, crowded with thoughts, faces, impulses, pleasures, obligations, and hopes. How does one travel in that city? How does one think in the crowded city that is life?

My basic belief about this is that I don't like to ride in taxicabs. Does that sound silly? Let me put it this way. Life is a journey; it's a ride from here to there. You step out of a door and you go to a door. There's a clock ticking in front of you that measures off your time. You are charged with that time. You don't know 'til the end of the trip what the charge will be. You step out of the cab and say good-bye to the driver, or you just walk away, that's all, the end of the trip.

How can this be a faith—not to ride in taxicabs? Let's consider the alternatives. You can ride in a cab, or you can ride in a subway. What about the subway? There, at least you're not alone. You get on the train, people bang into you, the train buckles and rolls, and the air is bad, it doesn't smell good, but life is going on there, and life doesn't smell good either. Yet somehow, it's wonderful.

In the car, there are lots of people, all kinds. Wholesome people, beautiful people, and sick, miserable, depraved people. Maybe you hear the squeak of some horrible music, a blind old woman with a disfigured face is led through the car by a little girl. The old woman is playing a mouth organ. People drop pennies in a tin cup the little girl holds up. Wedged in the corner of the car is a half-witted person babbling to himself. All these are a part of life—our comrades, our fellow wayfarers. Riding in a taxicab, one lacks of company.

The way I make the trip then can be my faith. Words don't count; it's what I do, and how I like to travel. When I pray, I can lock the door of an office and pray by myself. That's like riding in a cab. Or I can go to a church. I can pray in a temple or a cathedral, where thousands of people pass in and out every day. They are all praying, too. They are taking the same ride I am. And in mingling my prayers with them, I join the fellowship of the world, in humility before the mysteries that surround the journey. I think that is the way to take the ride.

NIVEN BUSCH *was an American novelist and screenwriter of such works as the acclaimed film* The Postman Always Rings Twice. *His novels include* Duel in the Sun, The Hate Merchant, *and* California Street. *At the age of eighty-five, Busch made his acting debut with a small part in* The Unbearable Lightness of Being.

There Is No Job More Important than Parenting

Benjamin Carson

THE SIMPLEST WAY TO SAY IT IS THIS: I believe in my mother.

My belief began when I was just a kid. I dreamed of becoming a doctor.

My mother was a domestic. Through her work, she observed that successful people spent a lot more time reading than they did watching television. She announced that my brother and I could only watch two to three preselected TV programs during the week. With our free time, we had to read two books each from the Detroit Public Library and submit to her written book reports. She would mark them up with check marks and highlights. Years later we realized her marks were a ruse. My mother was illiterate; she had only received a third-grade education.

Although we had no money, between the covers of those books I could go anywhere, do anything, and be anybody.

When I entered high school I was an A-student, but not for long. I wanted the fancy clothes. I wanted to hang out with the guys. I went from being an A-student to a B-student to a C-student, but I didn't care. I was getting the high fives and the low fives and the pats on the back. I was cool.

One night my mother came home from working her multiple jobs, and I complained about not having enough Italian knit shirts. She said, "Okay, I'll give you all the money I make this week scrubbing floors and cleaning bathrooms, and you can buy the family food and pay the bills. With everything left over, you can have all the Italian knit shirts you want."

I was very pleased with that arrangement, but once I got through allocating money, there was nothing left. I realized my mother was a financial genius to be able to keep a roof over our heads and any kind of food on the table, much less buy clothes.

I also realized that immediate gratification wasn't going to get me anywhere. Success required intellectual preparation.

I went back to my studies and became an A-student again, and eventually I fulfilled my dream and I became a doctor.

Over the years my mother's steadfast faith in God has inspired me, particularly when I had to perform extremely difficult surgical procedures or when I found myself faced with my own medical scare.

A few years ago I discovered I had a very aggressive form of prostate cancer; I was told it might have spread to my spine. My mother was steadfast in her faith in God. She never worried. She said that God was not through with me yet; there was no way that this was going to be a major problem. The abnormality in my spine turned out to be benign; I was able to have surgery and am cured.

My story is really my mother's story—a woman with little formal education or worldly goods who used her position as a parent to change the lives of many people around the globe. There is no job more important than parenting. This I believe.

DR. BENJAMIN CARSON *is director of pediatric neurosurgery at the Johns Hopkins Children's Center. His expertise includes separating conjoined twins and doing brain surgery to control seizures. A scholarship fund Carson founded has helped some 1,700 students through college. His mother is retired and lives with Carson and his family.*

A Journey toward Acceptance and Love

Greg Chapman

What do I believe? That the stories I tell myself shape my truth, my soul, and my life. I was raised to be a good Baptist and to be a patriotic American. I was raised to believe Catholics were idol-worshippers, liberals were communists, and that black and white never mixed. God filled the background, ready to condemn me into Hell. God saw everything bad about me, knew every wayward thought. I was born with original sin—I had no chance. At the same time, being a white American provided me a sense of privilege, of being one of the "better" people.

As I grew older, I began to struggle with my sexuality. Every day, I battled against demons driving me to impurity. I resisted and then I would succumb to unholy thought. I came to believe that I was an abomination, a thing hated by God. In search of a wife, I tried a dating service. Defeated, I waited for someone to take pity and love me. The idea of faking who I was to satisfy others turned my stomach. I came to believe that if I punished myself enough, God would show mercy and cure me of my wrongness.

I drove myself deep into depression. I remember my Bible group talking about how they kicked someone out for refusing to stop being gay. My blood chilled and my heart hiccupped. I remember my family asking me what was wrong with me. Why wasn't I dating? My sense of being less than fully human festered. I stopped going to church. I gave up on ever being loved. By age thirty-five, I had no more than a few hugs as the lifetime sum of my physical intimacy. My skin cried in deprivation. I had no hope except that one day things might improve if I endured. And then they did.

I started to change the basic stories of my life: that I'm bad, alienated from God, a freak of nature. I started to love myself and to believe the Divine did so as well. As that belief strengthened through the repetition of story, I began to love others, and I was loved back. The racism I grew up with faded. The more I loved myself, the more beauty I saw in everyone else. The more I healed, the more I viewed the Bible and all of our great myths as stories told by others, and I looked more and more to my heart to find the right one for me.

In six months, I joined with my life partner of five years and counting, became an Episcopalian, and replanted my political beliefs. And this I believe: The right story is the one that helps me to love myself the most, to create the most, to love others and to support them in their creations. For it is for those awesome experiences that I believe we are here. So I'm gay. And now, after decades of struggle, I tell a good story about it.

> GREG CHAPMAN *lives a few miles from the Houston hospital where he was born. A corporate tax accountant by profession, Chapman also enjoys writing and is working on a novel. He says composing his essay was a healing experience because it helped him explore the defining moments of his life.*

A Shared Moment of Trust

WARREN CHRISTOPHER

ONE NIGHT RECENTLY, I WAS DRIVING DOWN a two-lane highway at about sixty miles an hour. A car approached from the opposite direction, at about the same speed. As we passed each other, I caught the other driver's eye for only a second.

I wondered whether he might be thinking, as I was, how dependent we were on each other at that moment. I was relying on him not to fall asleep, not to be distracted by a cell phone conversation, not to cross over into my lane and bring my life suddenly to an end. And though we had never spoken a word to one another, he relied on me in just the same way.

Multiplied a million times over, I believe that is the way the world works. At some level, we all depend upon one another. Sometimes that dependence requires us simply to refrain from doing something, like crossing over the double yellow line. And sometimes it requires us to act cooperatively, with allies or even with strangers.

Back in 1980, I was negotiating for the release of the fifty-two Americans held hostage in Iran. The Iranians refused to meet with me face-to-face, insisting instead that we send messages back and forth through the government of Algeria. Although I had never before worked with the Algerian foreign minister, I had to rely on him to receive and transmit, with absolute accuracy, both the words and nuances of my messages. With his indispensable help, all fifty-two Americans came home safely.

As technology shrinks our world, the need increases for cooperative action among nations. In 2003, doctors in five nations were quickly mobilized to identify the SARS virus, an action that saved thousands of lives. The threat of international terrorism has shown itself to be a similar problem, one requiring coordinated action by police and intelligence forces across the world. We must recognize that our fates are not ours alone to control.

In my own life, I've put great stock in personal responsibility. But, as the years have passed, I've also come to believe that there are moments when one must rely upon the good faith and judgment of others. So, while each of us faces—at one time or another—the prospect of driving alone down a dark road, what we must learn with experience is that the approaching light may not be a threat, but a shared moment of trust.

WARREN CHRISTOPHER *was U.S. secretary of state from 1993 to 1997. As President Carter's deputy secretary of state, he helped normalize relations with China, win ratification of the Panama Canal treaties, and gain release of the American hostages in Iran. A native of North Dakota, Christopher now lives near Los Angeles.*

The Hardest Work You Will Ever Do

Mary Cook

The day my fiancé fell to his death, it started to snow, just like any November day, just like the bottom hadn't fallen out of my world when he freefell off the roof. His body, when I found it, was lightly covered with snow. It snowed almost every day for the next four months, while I sat on the couch and watched it pile up.

One morning, I shuffled downstairs and was startled to see a snowplow clearing my driveway and the bent back of a woman shoveling my walk. I dropped to my knees, crawled through the living room and back upstairs so those good Samaritans would not see me. I was mortified. My first thought was, how would I ever repay them? I didn't have the strength to brush my hair, let alone shovel someone's walk.

Before Jon's death, I took pride in the fact that I rarely asked for help or favors. I defined myself by my competence and independence. So who was I if I was no longer capable and busy? How could I respect myself if all I did was sit on the couch every day and watch the snow fall?

Learning how to receive the love and support that came my way wasn't easy. Friends cooked for me, and I cried because I couldn't even help them set the table. "I'm not usually this lazy," I wailed. Finally, my friend Kathy sat down with me and said, "Mary, cooking for you is not a chore. I love you and I want to do it. It makes me feel good to be able to do something for you."

Over and over, I heard similar sentiments from the people who supported me during those dark days. One very wise man told me, "You are not doing nothing. Being fully open to your grief may be the hardest work you will ever do."

I am not the person I once was, but in many ways I have changed for the better. The fabric of my life is now woven with gratitude and humility. I have been surprised to learn that there is incredible freedom that comes from facing one's worst fear and walking away whole. I believe there is strength in surrender.

> MARY COOK works on the ground crew for an air taxi company in Gustavus, Alaska, a community of four hundred surrounded by Glacier Bay National Park. In addition to loading and unloading planes, Cook handles the mail and tends the town's only coffeehouse. She also serves as a hospice volunteer.

Good Can Be as Communicable as Evil

Norman Corwin

Years ago, while watching a baseball game on television, I saw Orel Hershiser, pitching for the Dodgers, throw a fastball that hit a batter. The camera was on a close-up of Hershiser, and I could read his lips as he mouthed, "I'm sorry." The batter, taking first base, nodded to the pitcher in a friendly way and the game went on.

Just two words, and I felt good about Hershiser and the batter and the game all at once. It was only a common courtesy, but it made an impression striking enough for me to remember after many summers.

The blood relatives of common courtesy are kindness,

sympathy, and consideration. And the reward for exercising them is to feel good about having done so. When a motorist at an intersection signals to another who's waiting to join the flow of traffic, "Go ahead, it's okay, move in," and the recipient of the favor smiles and makes a gesture of appreciation, the giver enjoys a glow of pleasure. It's a very little thing, but it represents something quite big. Ultimately it's related to compassion, a quality in very short supply lately—and getting scarcer.

But look, let's not kid ourselves. It would be foolish to hope that kindness, consideration, and compassion will right wrongs, and heal wounds, and keep the peace, and set the new century on a course to recover from inherited ills. That would be asking a lot from even a heaven-sent methodology, and heaven is not in that business.

It comes down to the value of examples, which can be either positive or negative, and it works like this: Because of the principle that a calm sea and prosperous voyage do not make news but a shipwreck does, most circulated news is bad news. The badness of it is publicized, and the negative publicity attracts more of the same through repetition and imitation.

But good can be as communicable as evil, and that is where kindness and compassion come into play. So long as conscionable and caring people are around, so long as they are not muted or exiled, so long as they remain alert in thought and action, there is a chance for contagions of the right stuff, whereby democracy becomes no longer a choice of lesser evils, whereby the right to vote is not betrayed by staying away from the polls, whereby the freedoms of speech, assembly, religion, and dissent are never forsaken.

But why linger? Why wait to begin planting seeds, however long they take to germinate? It took us two hundred-plus years to get into the straits we now occupy, and it may take us as long again to get out, but there must be a beginning.

Norman Corwin's 1945 production, On a Note of Triumph, about the end of World War II in Europe, is considered a radio masterpiece. Now in his nineties, Corwin continues to teach writing and journalism at the University of Southern California. His living room holds broadcast memorabilia alongside his baseball souvenirs.

A Daily Walk Just to Listen

Susan Cosio

SOMETIMES I FEEL LIKE I HAVE NO REAL sense of direction. At forty-five, this is a little scary. I think my distraction is due to the variety of roles I play and my tendency to try to please others. Much of my day is spent responding to requests. "Mommy, will you . . . "; "Susan, can you . . ." My world is full of spoken and unspoken expectations that I try to live up to: as a parent, as a person, as a friend.

I believe I have to remove myself from the voices that barrage me in order to find my true compass. This includes a daily walk just to listen. The guiding light of my life is the still, small voice of the Holy Spirit. In our hectic, noisy world, I have to slow down or withdraw in order to hear it. Prayer, I have discovered, is less about what I say and more about what I hear.

Time set apart with God is like a hike to a peak from the middle of a dense forest; it gives me perspective, and some ability to see where I've been and where I am going.

Discerning God's voice is not so hard when I make time to listen closely. Sometimes I hear it as a sudden insight when I step back from a situation. Other times, it's a deep sense of my priorities, or a conviction about something I should do or say. I often take a walk with a pencil and notepad in my pocket, and return with notes for a speech or piece of writing. Later, someone tells me she was moved by the words I'd scribbled on that paper, and I know my prompting came from God.

My pursuit of spiritual truth is not about religion as much as it is about relationship. It is not about intellectualizing God's commands, but about internalizing his truth within my heart as well as my head, an understanding so deep and intimate that it affects not only my thinking, but my behavior as well. On my daily walks I've recognized how to parent my children through difficult situations, been prompted to call a friend I hadn't heard from in a while, and felt compelled to reach out to strangers—who soon became my friends.

I believe in a daily walk to listen because that is when I am close to God, that is when I find my way. And I am most at peace when I tune out the voices of the world long enough to hear the still, small voice of God directing me. "Be still," Psalm 46 reminds me, "and know that I am God."

> SUSAN COSIO *is a chaplain at Sutter Medical Center in Sacramento, California. A mother of three, she also writes feature articles for* The Davis Enterprise. *Cosio's favorite places to walk are in the mountains or on the beach, as well as through a bird sanctuary near her home.*

The Elusive Yet Holy Core

Kathy Dahlen

I entered college in the early 1970s, and my belief in God and Christ were intact. But it was through an unlikely class that I became convinced beyond dogma of a powerful truth.

Since I was an English major, I immersed myself in ideas and philosophies. But somewhere between Wordsworth's nature poems and Kafka's existential short stories, I felt a need to study something tangible—something in the world of blood, bones, and cells.

So, I signed up for the class "Human Anatomy and Physiology 101." As part of the coursework, our professor took us to an autopsy so we could see firsthand what had so far been limited to textbooks and drawings.

When we entered the morgue, our voices dropped to whispers, our eyes drawn to the human parts preserved in jars lining the walls.

In the autopsy room, a male body lay on a stainless-steel table. His skin was a waxy yellow, sunken, almost plastic. His mouth gaped.

He was a suicide.

The physician made a bloodless incision. A couple students on the outer rim of the group fainted; I managed to keep my ground and edged closer. There, inside, just as we had been taught, were the heart with its ventricles, the stomach still smelling of yeast, the bony frame, the paper-thin coils of intestine.

For some reason, it struck me that all these parts and pieces didn't explain fear or lust, ambition or love. There wasn't an organ I could probe to uncover kindness, or some tissue I could explore to find human will, or the drive to make music.

The doctor folded back a part of the man's scalp and, with an electric saw, cut carefully through the skull. The brain lay exposed as though in a cocoon, creased and wrinkled by thoughts and experiences.

Gazing at that mass of gray nerve tissue, I was unable to

reconcile the evidences I had known of self-sacrifice and forgiveness, or even this suicide, with the notion that a human life consists only of one's biology. I know myself well enough to admit to yearnings, imaginings, and thoughts that can't be reduced to chemical reactions or electric impulses.

The class, and particularly the autopsy experience, had taken me deeper than I anticipated. I had entered the study of the human body expecting to learn of our concrete physical existence. Instead, I discovered in a more profound way the human body as transitory and fragile and, by contrast, the soul as enduring.

This elusive, yet holy core whispers to me of God, of my ability to know and enjoy Him. It compels me to look beneath the surface, to remind myself that, like me, the lady next door who scowls on her way to the mailbox, or the kids who strut down the street, or my atheist friend who enjoys a good conversation, each bear an undying soul and deserve compassion.

KATHY DAHLEN has wanted to be a writer since her seventh-grade teacher inspired her to love language. A freelance writer, she is also a volunteer tutor in English as a second language. Dahlen lives in Sequim, Washington, a village on the northern coast of the Olympic peninsula.

My Father's Evening Star

WILLIAM O. DOUGLAS,
AS FEATURED IN THE 1950S SERIES

During moments of sadness or frustration, I often think of a family scene years ago in the town of Yakima, Washington. I was about seven or eight years old at the time. Father had died a few years earlier. Mother was sitting in the living room talking to me, telling me what a wonderful man Father was. She told me of his last illness and death. She told me of his departure from Cleveland, Washington, to Portland, Oregon, for what proved to be a fatal operation. His last words to her were these: "If I die, it will be glory; if I live, it will be grace."

I remember how those words puzzled me. I could not

understand why it would be glory to die. It would be glory to live, that I could understand. But why it would be glory to die was something I did not understand until later.

Then one day in a moment of great crisis, I came to understand the words of my father: "If I die, it will be glory; if I live, it will be grace." That was his evening star—the faith in a power greater than man. That was the faith of our fathers. A belief in a God who controlled man in the universe, that manifested itself in different ways to different people. It was written by scholars and learned men in dozens of different creeds. But riding high above all secular controversies was a faith in One who was the Creator, the Giver of Life, the Omnipotent.

Man's age-long effort has been to be free. Throughout time he has struggled against some form of tyranny that would enslave his mind or his body. So far in this century, three epidemics of it have been let loose in the world.

We can keep our freedom through the increasing crisis of history only if we are self-reliant enough to be free. Dollars, guns, and all the wondrous products of science and the machine will not be enough. "This night thy soul shall be required of thee."

These days I see graft and corruption reach high into government. These days I see people afraid to speak their minds because someone will think they are unorthodox and therefore disloyal. These days I see America identified more and more with material things, less and less with spiritual standards. These days I see America drifting from the Christian faith, acting abroad as an arrogant, selfish, greedy nation, interested only in guns and dollars, not in people and their hopes and aspirations. These days the words of my father come back to me more and more.

We need his faith, the faith of our fathers. We need a faith that dedicates us to something bigger and more important than ourselves or our possessions. Only if we have that faith will we be able to guide the destiny of nations, in this the most critical period of world history. This I believe.

WILLIAM O. DOUGLAS *was an associate justice of the U.S. Supreme Court from 1939 to 1975. As a boy, he hiked the Cascade Mountains near his home in Washington to strengthen legs weakened by polio. His opinions were characterized by a fierce commitment to individual rights and a distrust of government power.*

An Honest Doubter

~~~~~~

Elizabeth Deutsch (Earle),
as featured in the 1950s series

At the age of sixteen, many of my friends have already chosen a religion to follow (usually that of their parents) and are bound to it by many ties. I am still "freelancing" in religion, searching for beliefs to guide me when I am an adult. I fear I shall always be searching, never attaining ultimate satisfaction, for I possess that blessing and curse—a doubting, questioning mind.

At present, my doubting spirit has found comfort in certain ideas, gleaned from books and experience, to form a personal philosophy. I find that this philosophy—a code consisting of a few phrases—supplements, but does not replace, religion.

The one rule that could serve anyone in almost any situation is, "To see what must be done and not to do it, is a crime." Urged on by this, I volunteer for distasteful tasks or pick up scrap paper from the floor. I am no longer able to ignore duty without feeling guilty. This is "the still, small voice," to be sure, but sharpened by my own discernment of duty.

"The difficult we do at once, the impossible takes a little longer." This is the motto of a potential scientist, already struggling to unravel the mysteries of life. It rings with the optimism youth needs in order to stand up against trouble or failure.

Jonathan Edwards, a Puritan minister, resolved never to do anything out of revenge. I am a modern, a member of a church far removed from Puritanism, yet I have accepted this resolution. Since revenge and retaliation seem to have been accepted by nations today, I sometimes have difficulty reconciling my moral convictions with the tangled world being handed down to us by the adults. Apparently what I must do to make life more endurable is to follow my principles, with the hope that enough of this feeling will rub off on my associates to begin a chain reaction.

To a thinking person, such resolutions are very valuable;

nevertheless, they often leave a vacuum in the soul. Churches are trying to fill this vacuum, each by its own method. During this year, I have visited churches ranging from orthodoxy to extreme liberalism. In my search for a personal faith, I consider it my duty to expose myself to all forms of religion. Each church has left something within me—either a new concept of God and man, or an understanding and respect for those of other beliefs. I have found such experiences with other religions the best means for freeing myself from prejudices.

Through my visits, the reasoning of fundamentalists has become clearer to me, but I am still unable to accept it. I have a simple faith in the Deity and a hope that my attempts to live a decent life are pleasing to Him. If I were to discover that there is no afterlife, my motive for moral living would not be destroyed. I have enough of the philosopher in me to love righteousness for its own sake.

This is my youthful philosophy, a simple, liberal, and optimistic feeling, though I fear I may lose some of it as I become more adult. Already, the thought that the traditional thinkers might be right, after all, and I wrong, has made me waver. Still, these are my beliefs at sixteen. If I am mistaken, I am too young to realize my error. Sometimes, in a moment of mental despair, I think of the words "God loves an honest doubter" and am comforted.

Have I Learned Anything Important Since I Was Sixteen?

~~~~~

ELIZABETH DEUTSCH EARLE

OVER FIFTY YEARS AGO, AT THE AGE OF SIXTEEN, I wrote an essay published in the original *This I Believe* series. Since then I've advanced through much of the life cycle, including college, marriage to the same man for over forty years, two daughters, plus a scientific career, two lively grandsons, and death of parents and friends.

I still believe most of what I wrote long ago. Many of my early traits remain, including skepticism about religious authority, curiosity about the world, and the lofty desire to live a righteous life. The world I see now worries me at least as much as it did in the 1950s.

So, have I learned anything important since I was sixteen?

I now know that life is very often unfair. My own life has gone well, with much happiness and no exceptional grief or pain. Yet travel to other countries, experiences closer at hand, and just reading the news show me how hard things are for many people. That contrast troubles me, and I'm still not sure how best to respond to it. I do believe that those of us who have prospered should view our good fortune not as an indication of personal merit or entitlement, but as an obligation to recognize the needs of others.

Sadly, I've fallen short of my optimistic youthful goal of "doing what must be done." I try to be a good friend to the people I know and support causes with broader goals that I respect, but I recognize that my efforts have changed the world only in small ways.

Being a kind person and striving for social justice remain high priorities for me, but not for religious reasons. The "simple faith in the Deity" expressed in my teenage essay has faded over the years. Still, after the events of 9/11, I returned to the Unitarian Church, the same denomination in which I was active when I was sixteen. I've come to appreciate once again that communal reflection about life's deeper matters is sustaining and uplifting and provides a consistent nudge in worthy directions.

I believe that it's good to spend time engaged in the

present. I recently heard and admired the phrase "wherever you are, be there." This may not work for everyone; dissociating from misery may be wise. But someone like me, who focuses on lists of the next day's tasks and often reads a newspaper while walking outdoors, should remember also to look up at the sky and at the people around me.

I believe that it's important to recognize and appreciate joy when you feel it. Every once in a while, and not just on special occasions, I've suddenly realized that I am truly happy *right now*. This is a precious experience, one to savor.

When I was young, an honest and moral life seemed like a straightforward goal. I now know that it's not always easy to see what should be done and even harder actually to do it. Nevertheless I'm grateful that I still have some time to keep trying to get it right, and to savor each remaining day in my life.

When ELIZABETH DEUTSCH EARLE *was sixteen, she won a* This I Believe *essay contest in her hometown of Cleveland. Her prize was a trip to New York City to record her essay for broadcast on the original series. Today, Earle is a professor of plant breeding at Cornell University.*

An Ideal of Service to Our Fellow Man

~~~

ALBERT EINSTEIN,
AS FEATURED IN THE 1950S SERIES

THE MOST BEAUTIFUL THING WE CAN EXPERIENCE is the mysterious—the knowledge of the existence of something unfathomable to us, the manifestation of the most profound reason coupled with the most brilliant beauty. I cannot imagine a god who rewards and punishes the objects of his creation, or who has a will of the kind we experience in ourselves. I am satisfied with the mystery of life's eternity and with the awareness of—and glimpse into—the marvelous construction of the existing world together with the steadfast determination to comprehend a portion, be it ever so tiny, of the reason that manifests itself in nature. This is the basis of cosmic religiosity, and it appears to me that the most important function of art and science is to awaken this feeling among the receptive and keep it alive.

I sense that it is not the State that has intrinsic value in the machinery of humankind, but rather the creative, feeling individual, the personality alone that creates the noble and sublime.

Man's ethical behavior should be effectively grounded on compassion, nurture, and social bonds. What is moral is not of the divine, but rather a purely human matter, albeit the most important of all human matters. In the course of history, the ideals pertaining to human beings' behavior toward each other and pertaining to the preferred organization of their communities have been espoused and taught by enlightened individuals. These ideals and convictions—results of historical experience, empathy, and the need for beauty and harmony—have usually been willingly recognized by human beings, at least in theory.

The highest principles for our aspirations and judgments are given to us westerners in the Jewish-Christian religious tradition. It is a very high goal: free and responsible development of the individual, so that he may place his powers freely and gladly in the service of all mankind.

The pursuit of recognition for its own sake, an almost fanatical love of justice, and the quest for personal independence form the traditional themes of the Jewish people, of which I am a member.

But if one holds these high principles clearly before one's eyes and compares them with the life and spirit of our times, then it is glaringly apparent that mankind finds itself at present in grave danger. I see the nature of the current crises in the juxtaposition of the individual to society. The individual feels more than ever dependent on society, but he feels this dependence not in the positive sense, cradled, connected as part of an organic whole; he sees it as a threat to his natural rights, and even his economic existence. His position in society, then, is such that that which drives his ego is encouraged and developed, and that which would drive him toward other men—a weak impulse to begin with—is left to atrophy.

It is my belief that there is only one way to eliminate these evils, namely, the establishment of a planned economy coupled with an education geared toward social goals. Alongside the development of individual abilities, the education of the individual aspires to revive an ideal that is geared toward the service of our fellow man, and that needs to take the place of the glorification of power and outer success.

Albert Einstein

> ALBERT EINSTEIN *published his general theory of relativity in 1916, profoundly affecting the study of physics and cosmology for years. He won the Nobel Prize in Physics in 1921 for his work on the photoelectric effect. Einstein taught for many years at the Institute for Advanced Study at Princeton.*

The Power and Mystery of Naming Things

Eve Ensler

I BELIEVE IN THE POWER AND MYSTERY of naming things. Language has the capacity to transform our cells, rearrange our learned patterns of behavior, and redirect our thinking. I believe in naming what's right in front of us because that is often what is most invisible.

Think about the word "vagina." I believe that by saying it 128 times each show, night after night, naming my shame, exorcising my secrets, revealing my longing, was how I came back into my self, into my body. By saying it often enough and loud enough in places where it was not supposed to be said, the saying of it became both political and mystical and gave birth to a worldwide movement to end violence against women. The public utterance of a banished word, which represented a buried, neglected, dishonored part of the body was a door opening, an energy exploding, a story unraveling.

When I was finally able as an adult to sit with my mother and name the specific sexual and physical violence my father had perpetrated on me as a child, it was an impossible moment. It was the naming, the saying of what had actually happened in her presence, that lifted my twenty-year depression. By remaining silent, I had muted my experience, denied it, pushed it down. This had flattened my entire life. I believe it was this moment of naming that allowed both my mother and me to eventually face our deepest demons and deceptions and become free.

I think of women naming the atrocities committed against them by the Taliban in Afghanistan or women telling of the systematic rapes during the Bosnian war or just recently in Sri Lanka after the tsunami—women lining up in refugee camps to name their nightmares and losses and needs. I have traveled through this world and listened as woman after woman tells of being date-raped, or acid burned, genitally mutilated, beaten by her boyfriend, or molested by her stepfather.

Of course the stories are incredibly painful. But I believe as each woman tells her story for the first time, she breaks the silence, and by doing so breaks her isolation, begins to melt her shame and guilt, making her experience real, lifting her pain.

I believe one person's declaration sparks another and then another. Helen Caldicott naming the consequences of an escalating nuclear arms race gave rise to an antinuclear movement. The brave soldier who came forward and named the abuses at Abu Ghraib Prison was responsible for a sweeping investigation.

Naming things, breaking through taboos and denial is the most dangerous, terrifying, and crucial work. This has to happen in spite of political climates or coercions, in spite of careers being won or lost, in spite of the fear of being criticized, outcast, or disliked. I believe freedom begins with naming things. Humanity is preserved by it.

EVE ENSLER *is a writer and activist living in New York. Her play* The Vagina Monologues *has been translated into thirty-five languages and was performed more than two thousand times in 2004 alone. Ensler is founder of V-Day, an organization supporting efforts to end violence against women and girls worldwide.*

A Goal of Service to Humankind

Anthony Fauci

I BELIEVE I HAVE A PERSONAL RESPONSIBILITY to make a positive impact on society. I've tried to accomplish this goal by choosing a life of public service. I am a physician and a scientist confronting the challenge of infectious diseases. I consider my job a gift. It allows me to try and help alleviate the suffering of humankind.

I have three guiding principles that anchor my life, and I think about them every day.

First, I have an unquenchable thirst for knowledge. Knowledge goes hand-in-hand with truth—something I learned with a bit of tough love from my Jesuit education, first at Regis High School in New York City and then at Holy Cross College in Worcester, Massachusetts. I consider myself a perpetual student. You seek and learn every day: from an experiment in the lab, from reading a scientific journal, from taking care of a patient. Because of this, I rarely get bored.

Second, I believe in striving for excellence. I sweat the big and the small stuff! I do not apologize for this. One of the by-products of being a perfectionist and constantly trying to improve myself are sobering feelings of low-grade anxiety and a nagging sense of inadequacy. But this is not anxiety without a purpose. No, this anxiety keeps me humble. It creates a healthy tension that serves as the catalyst that drives me to fulfill my limited potential.

This has made me a better physician and scientist. Without this tension, I wouldn't be as focused.

I have accepted that I will never know or understand as much as I want. This is what keeps the quest for knowledge exciting! And it is one of the reasons I would do my job even if I did not get paid to come to work every day.

Third, I believe that as a physician my goal is to serve humankind.

I have spent all of my professional life in public service, most of it involved in research, care of patients, and public health policy concerning the HIV-AIDS epidemic. When I chose to concentrate on AIDS in the 1980s, many of my colleagues thought I was misguided to be focusing all of my attention on what was then considered "just a gay man's disease." But I felt that this was my destiny and was perfectly matched to my training. I knew deep down that this was going to become a public health catastrophe. I am committed to confronting the enormity of this global public health catastrophe and its potential for even greater devastation.

Failure to contain it cannot be an option. I believe that to be even marginally successful in working to contain this terrible disease, I must be guided by these principles. I must continually thirst for knowledge, accept nothing short of excellence, and know that the good of the global society is more important and larger than I am.

As a boy, DR. ANTHONY FAUCI *delivered prescriptions by bicycle for his father's drugstore. Currently director of the National Institute of Allergy and Infectious Diseases, his research focuses on HIV/AIDS, asthma, allergies, and other ailments. He advises the government on the global AIDS crisis and threats related to bioterrorism.*

The God Who Embraced Me

John W. Fountain

I BELIEVE IN GOD. Not that cosmic, intangible spirit-in-the-sky that Mama told me as a little boy "always was and always will be." But the God who embraced me when Daddy disappeared from our lives—from my life at age four—the night police led him away from our front door, down the stairs in handcuffs.

The God who warmed me when we could see our breath inside our freezing apartment, where the gas was disconnected in the dead of another wind-whipped Chicago winter, and there was no food, little hope, and no hot water.

The God who held my hand when I witnessed boys in

my 'hood swallowed by the elements, by death, and by hopelessness; who claimed me when I felt like "no-man's son," amid the absence of any man to wrap his arms around me and tell me, "everything's going to be okay," to speak proudly of me, to call me son.

I believe in God, God the Father, embodied in his Son Jesus Christ. The God who allowed me to feel His presence—whether by the warmth that filled my belly like hot chocolate on a cold afternoon, or that voice, whenever I found myself in the tempest of life's storms, telling me (even when I was told I was "nothing") that I was *something*, that I was His, and that even amid the desertion of the man who gave me his name and his DNA and little else, I might find in Him sustenance.

I believe in God, the God who I have come to know as father; as Abba—Daddy. I always envied boys I saw walking hand-in-hand with their fathers. I thirsted for the conversations fathers and sons have about the birds and the bees, or about nothing at all—simply feeling his breath, heartbeat, presence. As a boy, I used to sit on the front porch watching the cars roll by, imagining that one day one would park and the man getting out would be *my daddy*. But it never happened.

When I was eighteen, I could find no tears that Alabama winter's evening in January 1979 as I stood finally—

face-to-face—with my father lying cold in a casket, his eyes sealed, his heart no longer beating, his breath forever stilled. Killed in a car accident, he died drunk, leaving me hobbled by the sorrow of years of fatherless-ness.

By then, it had been years since Mama had summoned the police to our apartment that night, fearing that Daddy might hurt her—hit her—again. Finally his alcoholism consumed what good there was of him until it swallowed him whole.

It wasn't until many years later, standing over my father's grave for a long overdue conversation, that my tears flowed. I told him about the man I had become. I told him about how much I wished he had been in my life. And I realized fully that in his absence, I had found another. Or that *He— God, the Father, God, my Father*—had found me.

JOHN W. FOUNTAIN *is a professor of journalism at the University of Illinois at Urbana-Champaign. He has been a reporter for the* Chicago Tribune *and the* Washington Post, *and a national correspondent for the* New York Times. *Fountain wrote* True Vine: A Young Black Man's Journey of Faith, Hope, and Clarity.

Unleashing the Power of Creativity

Bill Gates

I'VE ALWAYS BEEN AN OPTIMIST, and I suppose that is rooted in my belief that the power of creativity and intelligence can make the world a better place.

For as long as I can remember, I've loved learning new things and solving problems. So when I sat down at a computer for the first time in seventh grade, I was hooked. It was a clunky old Teletype machine, and it could barely do anything compared to the computers we have today. But it changed my life.

When my friend Paul Allen and I started Microsoft

thirty years ago, we had a vision of "a computer on every desk and in every home," which probably sounded a little too optimistic at a time when most computers were the size of refrigerators. But we believed that personal computers would change the world. And they have.

And after thirty years, I'm still as inspired by computers as I was back in seventh grade.

I believe that computers are the most incredible tool we can use to feed our curiosity and inventiveness—to help us solve problems that even the smartest people couldn't solve on their own.

Computers have transformed how we learn, giving kids everywhere a window into *all* of the world's knowledge. They're helping us build communities around the things we care about, and to stay close to the people who are important to us, no matter where they are.

Like my friend Warren Buffett, I feel particularly lucky to do something every day that I love to do. He calls it "tap-dancing to work." My job at Microsoft is as challenging as ever, but what makes me "tap-dance to work" is when we show people something new, like a computer that can recognize your handwriting or your speech, or one that can store a lifetime's worth of photos, and they say, "I didn't know you could do that with a PC!"

But for all the cool things that a person can do with a PC, there are lots of other ways we can put our creativity and intelligence to work to improve our world. There are still far too many people in the world whose most basic needs go unmet. Every year, for example, millions of people die from diseases that are easy to prevent or treat in the developed world. Here in the United States, only one in three high school students graduates ready to go to college or hold down a good job.

I believe that my own good fortune brings with it a responsibility to give back to the world. My wife, Melinda, and I have committed to improving health and education in a way that can help as many people as possible.

As a father, I believe that the death of a child in Africa is no less poignant or tragic than the death of a child anywhere else. And that it doesn't take much to make an immense difference in these children's lives.

I'm still very much an optimist, and I believe that progress on even the world's toughest problems is possible—and it's happening every day. We're seeing new drugs for deadly diseases, new diagnostic tools, and new attention paid to the health problems in the developing world.

I'm excited by the possibilities I see for medicine, for education, and, of course, for technology. And I believe that through our natural inventiveness, creativity, and willingness to solve tough problems, we're going to make some amazing achievements in all these areas in my lifetime.

> BILL GATES *is chairman of Microsoft. He and his wife founded the Bill and Melinda Gates Foundation, which funds global health, education, and public library projects.*

The People Who Love You When No One Else Will

Cecile Gilmer

I BELIEVE THAT FAMILIES ARE NOT ONLY blood relatives but sometimes just people that show up and love you when no one else will.

In May 1977, I lived in a Howard Johnson's motel off of Interstate 10 in Houston. My dad and I shared a room with two double beds and a bathroom way too small for a modest fifteen-year-old girl and her father. Dad's second marriage was in trouble, and my stepmother had kicked us both out of the house the previous week. Dad had no idea what to do with me. And that's when my other family showed up.

Barbara and Roland Beach took me into their home because their only daughter, Su, my best friend, asked them to. I lived with them for the next seven years.

Barb starched my drill team skirts same as Su's. She made sure I had lunch money, doctors' appointments, help with homework, Jordache jeans, puka shell necklaces, and nightly hugs. Barbara and Roland attended every football game where Su and I marched, every drama performance I was in, even when I had no speaking lines. As far as I could tell, for the Beaches, there was no difference between Su and me: I was their daughter, too.

When Su and I left for rival colleges, they kept my room the same for the entire four years I attended school. Recently, Barb presented me with an insurance policy they bought when I first moved in with them and had continued to pay on for twenty-three years.

The Beaches knew all about me when they took me in. When I was seven, my mother died of a self-inflicted gunshot wound and from then on my father relied on other people to raise his kids. By the time I went to live with the Beaches, I believed that life was entirely unfair and that love was tenuous and untrustworthy. I believed that the only person who would take care of me was me.

Without the Beaches, I would have become a bitter, cynical woman. They gave me a home that allowed me to grow and change. They kept me from being paralyzed by my past, and they gave me the confidence to open my heart.

I believe in family. For me, it wasn't the family that was there on the day I was born, but the one that was there for me when I was living in a Howard Johnson's on Interstate 10.

> Cecile Gilmer *has moved twenty-six times since her birth in San Antonio in 1962. She now lives with her cat and dog in Logan, Utah, where she is an events planner. Gilmer is still close to her friends Su and the Beaches, having recently joined them for a family reunion.*

The Willingness to Work for Solutions

Newt Gingrich

I BELIEVE THAT THE WORLD IS INHERENTLY a very dangerous place and that things that are now very good can go bad very quickly.

I stood recently at Checkpoint Charlie and I saw where the Berlin Wall had once been, where millions had lived in slavery only twenty years ago, and I realized that it could happen again. I've stood at Auschwitz, where millions were massacred. Then I read about Darfur, where hundreds of thousands are dying in the Sudan.

I watch the bombings in Baghdad and I know they could be happening in Atlanta or in Washington. I look at civilizations that have collapsed: Rome, Greece, China, the Aztecs, the Mayas. And then I look around at our pretensions and our beliefs—that we are somehow permanent—and I am reminded that it is the quality of leaders, the courage of a people, the ability to solve problems that enables us to continue for one more year, and then one more year, until our children and our grandchildren have had this freedom, this safety, this health, and this prosperity.

I learned this belief from my stepfather, a career soldier who served America in the second World War, in Korea, and in Vietnam. When I was a child, we lived in France—a France that was still suffering from World War II bomb damage; a France that still had amputees from the first World War and special seats on the subway for those who had been wounded in the first and second World Wars; a France that was fighting a war in Algiers; a France that had 100 percent inflation.

We went to the battlefield of Verdun, the greatest battle of the first World War. We stayed with a friend of my father's who had been drafted, sent to the Philippines, served in the Bataan Death March, and spoke of three and a half years in a Japanese prison camp.

And suddenly, as a young man, I realized this is all real: The gap between our civilization, our prosperity, our freedoms, and all of those things is the quality of our leaders, the courage of our people, the willingness to face facts, and the willingness to work for solutions—solutions to energy, solutions to the environment, solutions to the economy, solutions to education, and solutions to national security. We have real challenges; we have a wonderful country. We need to keep it, and to keep it we're going to have to learn these kinds of lessons.

That's what I believe.

> *Former Georgia congressman* NEWT GINGRICH *was speaker of the U.S. House of Representatives from 1995 to 1999. His 1994 agenda, known as the "Contract with America," helped Republicans achieve their first House majority in forty years. When recording his essay, Gingrich discarded what he'd written and spoke this piece extemporaneously.*

The Connection between Strangers

Miles Goodwin

On June 23, 1970, I had just been mustered out of the Army after completing my one-year tour of duty in Vietnam. I was a twenty-three-year-old Army veteran on a plane from Oakland, California, returning home to Dallas, Texas.

I had been warned about the hostility many of our fellow countrymen felt toward returning Nam Vets at that time. There were no hometown parades for us when we came home from that unpopular war. Like tens of thousands of others, I was just trying to get home without incident.

I sat, in uniform, in a window seat, chain smoking and avoiding eye contact with my fellow passengers. No one was sitting in the seat next to me, which added to my isolation. A young girl, not more than ten years old, suddenly appeared in the aisle. She smiled and without a word timidly handed me a magazine. I accepted her offering, her quiet "welcome home." All I could say was, "Thank you." I do not know where she sat down or who she was with because right after accepting the magazine from her I turned to the window and wept. Her small gesture of compassion was the first I had experienced in a long time.

I believe in the connection between strangers when they reach out to one another.

That young girl undoubtedly has no memory of what happened years ago. I like to think of her as having grown up continuing to touch others and teaching her children to do the same. I know she might have been told to give me the "gift" by her mother. Her father might still have been in Vietnam at that point or maybe he had not survived the war. It doesn't matter why she gave me the magazine. The important thing is she did.

Since then, I have followed her example and tried, in different ways for different people, to do the same for them. Like me on that long-ago plane ride, they will never know why a stranger took the time to extend a hand. But I know that my attempts since then are all because of that little girl. Her offer of a magazine to a tired, scared, and lonely soldier has echoed throughout my life. I have to believe that my small gestures have the same effect on others. And to that little girl, now a woman, I would like to take this opportunity to say again, thank you.

> MILES GOODWIN *is a real estate attorney in Milwaukee. During the Vietnam War he was a clerk for the U.S. Army headquarters outside Saigon. Goodwin says it took about ten years after his discharge before he told people about his service there. He enjoys his family, investing, and riding motorcycles.*

An Athlete of God

Martha Graham,
as featured in the 1950s series

I BELIEVE THAT WE LEARN BY PRACTICE. Whether it means to learn to dance by practicing dancing or to learn to live by practicing living, the principles are the same. In each it is the performance of a dedicated precise set of acts, physical or intellectual, from which comes shape of achievement, a sense of one's being, a satisfaction of spirit. One becomes in some area an athlete of God.

Practice means to perform, over and over again in the face of all obstacles, some act of vision, of faith, of desire. Practice is a means of inviting the perfection desired.

I think the reason dance has held such an ageless magic

for the world is that it has been the symbol of the performance of living. Many times I hear the phrase "the dance of life." It is close to me for a very simple and understandable reason. The instrument through which the dance speaks is also the instrument through which life is lived: the human body. It is the instrument by which all the primaries of experience are made manifest. It holds in its memory all matters of life and death and love.

Dancing appears glamorous, easy, delightful. But the path to the paradise of that achievement is not easier than any other. There is fatigue so great that the body cries, even in its sleep. There are times of complete frustration; there are daily small deaths. Then I need all the comfort that practice has stored in my memory, and a tenacity of faith. But it must be the kind of faith that Abraham had, wherein he "staggered not at the promise of God through unbelief."

It takes about ten years to make a mature dancer. The training is twofold. There is the study and practice of the craft in order to strengthen the muscular structure of the body. The body is shaped, disciplined, honored, and, in time, trusted. The movement becomes clean, precise, eloquent, truthful. Movement never lies. It is a barometer telling the state of the soul's weather to all who can read it. This might be called the law of the dancer's life—the law which governs its outer aspects.

Then there is the cultivation of the being. It is through this that the legends of the soul's journey are retold with all their gaiety and their tragedy and the bitterness and sweetness of living. It is at this point that the sweep of life catches up the mere personality of the performer, and while the individual (the undivided one) becomes greater, the personal becomes less personal. And there is grace. I mean the grace resulting from faith: faith in life, in love, in people, and in the act of dancing. All this is necessary to any performance in life which is magnetic, powerful, rich in meaning.

In a dancer there is a reverence for such forgotten things as the miracle of the small beautiful bones and their delicate strength. In a thinker there is a reverence for the beauty of the alert and directed and lucid mind. In all of us who perform there is an awareness of the smile which is part of the equipment, or gift, of the acrobat. We have all walked the high wire of circumstance at times. We recognize the gravity pull of the earth as he does. The smile is there because he is practicing living at that instant of danger. He does not choose to fall.

In seven decades as a dancer and choreographer, MARTHA GRAHAM created 181 ballets. A founder of modern dance, she is known for her collaborations with other leading artists, including composer Aaron Copland. Graham's company trained dance greats such as Alvin Ailey and Twyla Tharp.

Seeing in Beautiful, Precise Pictures

Temple Grandin

Because I have autism, I live by concrete rules instead of abstract beliefs. And because I have autism, I think in pictures and sounds.

Here's how my brain works: It's like the search engine Google for images. If you say the word "love" to me, I'll surf the Internet inside my brain. Then, a series of images pops into my head. What I'll see is a picture of a mother horse with a foal; or I think of "Herbie, the Love Bug"; scenes from the movie *Love Story;* or the Beatles song "Love, love, all you need is love . . ."

When I was a child, my parents taught me the difference

between good and bad behavior by showing me specific examples. My mother told me that you don't hit other kids because you would not like it if they hit you. That makes sense. But, if my mother told me to be "nice" to someone—it was too vague for me to comprehend. But if she said that being nice meant delivering daffodils to a next-door neighbor, that I could understand.

I believe that doing practical things can make the world a better place. When I was in my twenties, I thought a lot about the meaning of life. At the time, I was getting started in my career designing more humane facilities for animals at ranches and slaughterhouses. Many people would think that to even work at a slaughterhouse would be inhumane, but they forget that every human and animal eventually dies. In my mind, I had a picture of a way to make that dying as peaceful as possible.

Back in the 1970s, I went to fifty different feedlots and ranches in Arizona and Texas and helped them work cattle. I cataloged the parts of each facility that worked effectively. I took the best loading ramps, sorting pens, single-file chutes, crowd pens, and other components and assembled them into an ideal new system. I get great satisfaction when a rancher tells me that my corral design helps cattle move through it quietly and easily. When cattle stay calm, it means they are not scared. And that makes me feel I've accomplished something important.

Some people might think if I could snap my fingers I'd choose to be "normal." But, I wouldn't want to give up my ability to see in beautiful, precise pictures. I believe in them.

TEMPLE GRANDIN *is an associate professor of animal science at Colorado State University. She has designed one-third of all livestock handling facilities in the United States with the goal of decreasing the fear and pain animals experience in the slaughter process. Grandin is the author of* Thinking in Pictures *and* Animals in Translation: Using the Mysteries of Autism to Decode Animal Behavior.

Disrupting My Comfort Zone

Brian Grazer

I WAS FORTY-FIVE YEARS OLD when I decided to learn how to surf.

Picture the scene. The North Shore of Oahu. The toughest, most competitive surfing spot on the planet. Fourteen-foot swells. Twenty tattooed locals. And me, five feet, eight inches of abject terror. What will get me first, I wondered, the next big wave or the guy to my right with the tattoo on his chest that reads RIP?

They say life is tough enough. But I guess I like to make things difficult on myself, because I do that all the time. Every day. On purpose. That's because I believe in disrupting my comfort zone.

When I started out in the entertainment business, I made a list of people I thought it would be good to meet. Not people who could give me a job or a deal. But people who could shake me up, teach me something, challenge my ideas about myself and the world.

So I started calling up experts in all kinds of fields: trial lawyers, neurosurgeons, CIA agents, embryologists, firewalkers, police chiefs, hypnotists, forensic anthropologists, and even presidents. Some of them—like Carlos Castaneda, Jonas Salk, and Fidel Castro—were world-famous.

Of course, I didn't know any of these people, and none of them knew me. So when I called these people up to ask for a meeting, the response wasn't always friendly. And even when they agreed to give me some time, the results weren't always what one might describe as pleasant.

Take, for example, Edward Teller, the father of the hydrogen bomb. You've heard of him? However, he'd never heard of me. It took me a year of begging, cajoling, and more begging to get him to agree to meet with me. And then what happened? He ridiculed and insulted me. But that was okay. I was hoping to learn something from him— and I did, even if it was only that I'm not that interesting to a physicist with no taste for our pop culture.

Over the last thirty years, I've produced more than fifty movies and twenty television series. I'm successful and, in my business, pretty well-known. I'm a guy who could retire to the golf course tomorrow, where the worst that could happen is that my Bloody Mary is watered down. So why do I continue to subject myself to this sort of thing?

The answer is simple. Disrupting my comfort zone, bombarding myself with challenging people and situations, this is the best way I know to keep growing. And to paraphrase a biologist I once met, if you're not growing, you're dying.

So maybe I'm not the best surfer on the North Shore. But that's okay. The discomfort, the uncertainty, the physical and mental challenge I get from it—all the things that too many of us spend our time and energy trying to avoid—they're precisely the things that keep me in the game.

BRIAN GRAZER *is an Oscar-winning movie producer and an Emmy-winning television producer. He cofounded Imagine Entertainment with longtime friend, director Ron Howard, and together they created blockbusters including* The Da Vinci Code, A Beautiful Mind, Apollo 13, *and* Splash. *The Producers Guild of America honored Grazer with the David O. Selznick Lifetime Achievement Award in 2001.*

Science Nourishes the Mind and the Soul

Brian Greene

ONE DAY, WHEN I WAS ABOUT ELEVEN, walking back to Public School 87 in Manhattan after our class visit to the Hayden Planetarium, I became overwhelmed by a feeling I'd never had before. I was gripped by a hollow, pit-in-the-stomach sense that my life might not matter. I'd learned that our world is a rocky planet, orbiting one star among the one hundred billion others in our galaxy, which is but one of hundreds of billions of galaxies scattered throughout the universe. Science had made me feel small.

In the years since, my view of science and the role it can play in society and the world has changed dramatically.

While we are small, my decades of immersion in science convince me this is cause for celebration. From our lonely corner of the cosmos we have used ingenuity and determination to touch the very limits of outer and inner space. We have figured out fundamental laws of physics—laws that govern how stars shine and light travels, laws that dictate how time elapses and space expands, laws that allow us to peer back to the briefest moment after the universe began.

None of these scientific achievements has told us why we're here or given us the answer to life's meaning—questions science may never address. But just as our experience playing baseball is enormously richer if we know the rules of the game, the better we understand the universe's rules—the laws of physics—the more deeply we can appreciate our lives within it.

I believe this because I've seen it.

I've seen children's eyes light up when I tell them about black holes and the big bang. I've witnessed the self-worth and confidence a young student gains by completing even the simplest of mathematical calculations. I've spoken with high school dropouts who've stumbled upon books describing the amazing achievements of science and returned to their studies with purpose and zeal. I've received letters from young soldiers in Iraq, telling me how reading popular accounts of relativity and quantum physics has provided them hope that there is something larger, something universal that binds us together. Such is the capacity of science, not only to explain, but to inspire.

Which is why I am distressed when I meet students who approach science and math with drudgery. I know it doesn't have to be that way. But when science is presented as a collection of facts that need to be memorized, when math is taught as a series of abstract calculations without revealing its power to unravel the mysteries of the universe, it can all seem pointless and boring.

Even more troubling, I've encountered students who've been told they don't have the capacity to grasp math and science.

These are lost opportunities.

I believe we owe our young an education that captures the exhilarating drama of science.

I believe the process of going from confusion to understanding is a precious, even emotional, experience that can be the foundation of self-confidence. I believe that through its rational evaluation of truth and indifference to personal belief, science transcends religious and political divisions and so does bind us into a greater, more resilient whole.

I believe that the wonder of discovery can lift the spirit like Brahms's Third Symphony.

I believe that the breathtaking ideas of science can nourish not only the mind but also the soul.

A native New Yorker, BRIAN GREENE *teaches physics and mathematics at Columbia University. He is a proponent of string theory, which attempts to unify all the forces of nature into a single framework. He authored* The Fabric of the Cosmos *and* The Elegant Universe.

In Praise of the "Wobblies"

Ted Gup

For years I really didn't know what I believed. I always seemed to stand in the no-man's-land between opposing arguments, yearning to be won over by one side or the other, but finding instead degrees of merit in both.

I remember some thirty-five years ago, sitting at a table with the editor of the *Washington Post* and a half dozen Harvard kids. We were all finalists for a *Post* internship, and the editor was there to winnow our numbers down. He asked each of us what we thought about the hot issues of the day—Vietnam, Nixon, the demonstrations. The Harvard kids were dazzling. They knew exactly where they stood.

Me, I just stumbled on every issue, sounding so muddled. I was sure I had forever lost my shot at the *Post*. Why, I wondered, could I not see as clearly as those around me?

When the lunch was over and everyone rose to leave, the editor put his hand on my arm and asked me to stay. We talked again about the war and how it was dividing the country. A month later he wrote me a rejection letter. He said I was too young for the job but he liked my attitude. He told me that he "hunched I had a hell of a future" and to keep bugging him. I did.

Seven years later he hired me.

But that first letter, now framed in my office, had already given me an invaluable license. It had let me know that it was okay to be perplexed, to be torn by issues, to look at the world and not feel inadequate because it would not sort itself out cleanly. In the company of the confident, I had always envied their certainty. I imagined myself like some tiny sailboat, aimlessly tacking in whatever wind prevailed at the moment.

But in time, I came to accept, even embrace, what I called "my confusion," and to recognize it as a friend and ally, no apologies needed. I preferred to listen rather than to speak; to inquire, not crusade. As a noncombatant, I was welcomed at the tables of even bitterly divided foes. I came to recognize that I had my own compass and my own convictions, and if, at times, they took me in circles, at least they expanded outward. I had no wish for converts—where would I lead them?

An editor and mentor at the *Post* once told me I was "Wobbly." I asked who else was in that category and drew comfort from its quirky ranks. They were good people all—open-minded, inquisitive, and, yes, confused. We shared a common creed. Our articles of faith all ended with a question mark. I wouldn't want a whole newsroom, hospital, platoon, or—God forbid—a nation of us. But in periods of crisis, when passions are high and certainty runs rabid, it's good to have a few of us on hand. In such times, I believe it falls to us Wobblies to try and hold the shrinking common ground.

TED GUP *has written for* Time, National Geographic, *the* New York Times, *and other publications. He wrote* The Book of Honor: Covert Lives and Classified Deaths at the CIA *and teaches journalism at Case Western Reserve University.*

The Power of Presence

DEBBIE HALL

I BELIEVE IN THE POWER OF PRESENCE.

I was recently reminded of this belief when I and several other Red Cross volunteers met a group of evacuees from Hurricane Katrina. We were there, as mental health professionals, to offer "psychological first aid." Despite all the training in how to "debrief," to educate about stress reactions, and to screen for those needing therapy, I was struck again by the simple healing power of presence. Even as we walked in the gate to the shelter, we were greeted with a burst of gratitude from the first person we encountered. I felt appreciated, but somewhat guilty, because I hadn't really done anything yet.

Presence is a noun, not a verb; it is a state of being, not doing. States of being are not highly valued in a culture that places a high priority on doing. Yet, true presence or "being with" another person carries with it a silent power—to bear witness to a passage, to help carry an emotional burden, or to begin a healing process. In it, there is an intimate connection with another that is perhaps too seldom felt in a society that strives for ever-faster "connectivity."

I was first hurled into an ambivalent presence many years ago, when a friend's mother died unexpectedly. Part of me wanted to rush down to the hospital, but another part of me didn't want to intrude on this acute and very personal phase of grief. I was torn about what to do. Another friend with me at the time said, "Just go. Just be there." I did, and I will never regret it.

Since then I have not hesitated to be in the presence of others for whom I could "do" nothing. I sat at the bedside of a young man in a morphine coma to blunt the pain of his AIDS-related dying. We spoke to him about his inevitable journey out of this life. He later told his parents—in a brief moment of lucidity—that he had felt us with him.

Another time I visited a former colleague dying of

cancer in a local hospice. She, too, was not awake and presumably unaware of others' presence with her. The atmosphere was by no means solemn. Her family had come to terms with her passing and were playing guitars and singing. They allowed her to be present with them as though she were still fully alive.

With therapy clients, I am still pulled by the need to do more than be, yet repeatedly struck by the healing power of connection created by being fully there in the quiet understanding of another. I believe in the power of presence, and it is not only something we give to others. It always changes me—and always for the better.

> DEBBIE HALL *has been a psychologist in the Pediatrics Department of San Diego's Naval Medical Center for twelve years. She also volunteers for the Disaster Mental Health Team of her local Red Cross. A lifelong Californian, Hall lives in Escondido with five cats and a fifteen-year-old golden retriever.*

A Grown-Up Barbie

Jane Hamill

I CONSIDER MYSELF A FEMINIST, and I feel like a moron admitting it, but it's true: I believe in Barbie.

For me, as a kid, Barbie was about cool clothes, a cool job, cool friends, and cool accessories—the airplane, the apartment building, and the camper. I learned to sew so I could make outfits for Barbie and her friends, who took turns being the airplane pilot, the doctor, the fashion designer. Barbie was never about Ken. He was always a little dusty and in the corner. My Barbie didn't enter beauty contests, get married, or have children. She went to Paris and New York for fancy dinners and meetings.

Years later, I became a fashion designer. I lived in Paris and New York and went to fashion shows and fancy dinners. It was all about the outfits and I began to wonder: Am I just a grown-up Barbie? I am a strong, intelligent woman. My idols are supposed to be Georgia O'Keeffe or Gloria Steinem or Madeleine Albright. Am I in danger of becoming a puff piece like Barbie?

When I achieved my Barbie-style life, I wasn't so sure I wanted it. My husband is a prosecutor. He can change a person's life forever in just one day. I come home from work and say, "I sold a great green dress today and you should have *seen* the shoes!"

Today, I'm sort of the anti–fashion designer fashion designer. I don't particularly like shopping, and if someone says fashion is silly, I'm the first to agree. It's just clothes. But if the sleeve is cut just right, it makes a difference. It makes a difference in how you present yourself. So many people have body issues. I hope I can help people like themselves more.

Clothes are personal. And they're part of your identity. A few weeks ago, I got a call from a customer. She told me, now that she has my clothes to put on in the morning, she's never felt so confident in her life. They may just be clothes, but they help her to be who she wants to be and to believe in herself.

The blonde-haired, blue-eyed Malibu Barbie I loved looked nothing like my red-haired, freckled self. But that didn't stop me from thinking I was just like Barbie—cool and independent and smart. It's only as an adult that I realize that my belief in Barbie is really a belief in my own imagination, in whoever I imagined I could be, and whatever I imagined I could do. I believe in imagining a life, and then trying to live it.

JANE HAMILL *grew up designing and sewing clothes for family members in her hometown of Chicago. She studied fashion in New York and Paris before opening her own boutique at age twenty-five. Hamill is on the advisory board of Columbia College in Chicago and is a member of the Apparel Industry Board.*

Happy Talk

Oscar Hammerstein II,
as featured in the 1950s series

I have an unusual statement to make. I am a man who believes he is happy. What makes it unusual is that a man who is happy seldom tells anyone. The unhappy man is more communicative. He is eager to recite what is wrong with the world, and he seems to have a talent for gathering a large audience. It is a modern tragedy that *despair* has so many spokesmen, and *hope* so few.

I believe, therefore, that it is important for a man to announce that he is happy even though such an announcement is less dramatic and less entertaining than the cries of his pessimistic opposite. Why do I believe I am happy?

Death has deprived me of many whom I loved. Dismal failure has followed many of my most earnest efforts. People have disappointed me. I have disappointed them. I have disappointed myself.

Further than this, I am aware that I live under a cloud of international hysteria. The cloud could burst, and a rain of atom bombs could destroy millions of lives, including my own. From all this evidence, could I not build up a strong case to prove why I am not happy at all? I could, but it would be a false picture, as false as if I were to describe a tree only as it looks in winter. I would be leaving out a list of people I love, who have not died. I would be leaving out an acknowledgment of the many successes that have sprouted among my many failures. I would be leaving out the blessing of good health, the joy of walking in the sunshine. I would be leaving out my faith that the goodness in man will triumph eventually over the evil that causes war.

All these things are as much a part of my world as the darker worries that shade them. The conflict of good and bad merges in thick entanglement. You cannot isolate virtue and beauty and success and laughter, and keep them from all contact with wickedness and ugliness and failure and weeping. The man who strives for such isolated joy is riding for a fall. He will wind up in isolated gloom.

I don't believe anyone can enjoy living in this world

unless he can accept its imperfection. He must know and admit that he is imperfect, that all other mortals are imperfect, that it is childish to allow these imperfections to destroy all his hope and all his desire to live. Nature is older than man, and she is still far from perfect. Her summers do not always start promptly on June 21. Her bugs and beetles and other insects often go beyond her obvious intentions, devouring the leaves and buds with which she has adorned her countryside. After the land has remained too dry for too long, she sends relieving rains. But frequently they come in torrents so violent that they do more harm than good. Over the years, however, nature keeps going on in her imperfect way, and the result—in spite of her many mistakes—is a continuing miracle. It would be folly for an individual to seek to do better—to do better than to go on in his own imperfect way, making his mistakes, riding out the rough and bewildering, exciting and beautiful storm of life until the day he dies.

OSCAR HAMMERSTEIN II *wrote the book and lyrics for many operettas and musical comedies. He wrote* Show Boat *with composer Jerome Kern. Later, with composer Richard Rodgers, Hammerstein wrote some of his greatest musicals, including* Oklahoma!, South Pacific, The King and I, *and* The Sound of Music.

Natural Links in a Long Chain of Being

Victor Hanson

I believe we are not alone.

Even if I am on the other side of the world from the farmhouse I live in, I still dream of the ancient vines out the window, and the shed out back that my grandfather's father built in 1870 with eucalyptus trunks. As long as I can recreate these images, I never quite leave home.

I don't think farming in the same place for six generations is a dead weight that keeps you shackled, doing the identical thing year in and year out. Instead it is a rare link to others before me, who pruned the same vines and painted the same barn that I have. If those in this house survived the

Panic of 1893 or the Great Depression, or bathed with cold water and used an outhouse, then surely I know I can weather high gas prices.

I believe that all of us need some grounding in our modern world of constant moving, buying, selling, meeting, and leaving. Some find constancy in religion. Others lean on friends or community for permanence. But we need some daily signposts that we are not novel, not better, not worse from those who came before us.

For me, this house, this farm, these ancient vines, are those roots. Although I came into this world alone and will leave alone, I am not alone.

There are ghosts of dozens of conversations in the hallways, stories I remember about buying new plows that now rust in the barnyard, and ruined crops from the same vines that we are now harvesting.

I believe all of us are natural links in a long chain of being. I need to know what time of day it is, what season is coming, whether the wind is blowing north or from the east, and if the moon is still full tomorrow night, just as the farmers who came before me did.

The physical world around us changes constantly; human nature does not. We must struggle in our brief existence to find some transcendent meaning during reoccurring heartbreak and disappointment and so find solace in the knowledge that our ancestors have all gone through this before.

You may find all that too intrusive, living with the past as present. I find it exhilarating. I believe there is an old answer for every new problem—that wise whispers of the past are with us to assure us that if we just listen and remember, we are not alone; we have been here before.

> *Classics and military history scholar* Victor Hanson *is a professor emeritus at California State University, Fresno, and a senior fellow at the Hoover Institution. His family farm includes forty acres of seedless grapes grown for raisins. Hanson hopes his son, William, will succeed him in tending the farm.*

Talking with the Sun

Joy Harjo

I BELIEVE IN THE SUN. In the tangle of human failures of fear, greed, and forgetfulness, the sun gives me clarity. When explorers first encountered my people, they called us heathens, sun worshippers. They didn't understand that the sun is a relative and illuminates our path on this earth.

Many of us continue ceremonies that ensure a connection with the sun. After dancing all night in a circle we realize that we are a part of a larger sense of stars and planets dancing with us overhead. When the sun rises at the apex of the ceremony, we are renewed. There is no mistaking this connection, though Wal-Mart might be just down the road.

Humans are vulnerable and rely on the kindnesses of the earth and the sun; we exist together in a sacred field of meaning.

A few weeks ago I visited some friends at a pueblo for a feast day celebration. The runners were up at dawn and completed a ceremonial run that ensures that the sun will continue to return. It is a humble and necessary act of respect. And because the celebration continues, the sun, the earth, and these humans are still together in a harmonious relationship.

Our earth is shifting. We can all see it. I hear from my Inuit and Yupik relatives up north that everything has changed. It's so hot; there is not enough winter. Animals are confused. Ice is melting.

The quantum physicists have it right; they are beginning to think like Indians: Everything is connected dynamically at an intimate level. When you remember this, then the current wobble of the earth makes sense. How much more oil can be drained without replacement, without reciprocity?

One day recently, I walked out of a hotel room just off Times Square at dawn to find the sun. It was the fourth morning since the birth of my fourth granddaughter. This was the morning I was to present her to the sun, as a relative, as one of us. It was still dark, overcast as I walked through Times Square. I stood beneath a twenty-first-century totem pole of symbols of multinational corporations, made of flash and neon.

The sun rose up over the city, but I couldn't see it amidst the rain. Though I was not at home, bundling up the baby to carry her outside, I carried this newborn girl within the cradleboard of my heart. I held her up and presented her to the sun, so she would be recognized as a relative, so that she won't forget this connection, this promise, so that we all remember the sacredness of life.

> Joy Harjo *has written eight collections of poetry and has produced three CDs of her music and poetry. A native of Tulsa, Oklahoma, she is a member of the Muskogee Creek Nation. When not teaching creative writing at the University of New Mexico, or traveling and performing, Harjo lives in Honolulu.*

A Morning Prayer in a Little Church

Helen Hayes,
as featured in the 1950s series

Once, years ago, I got into a dogfight. I was wheeling a baby carriage, my pet cocker spaniel trotting beside me, and without warning, three dogs—an Afghan, a St. Bernard, and a Dalmatian—pounced on the cocker and started tearing him to pieces. I shrieked for help. Two men in a car stopped, looked, and drove on.

When I saw that, I was so infuriated that I waded in and stopped the fight myself. My theatrical training never stood me in better stead. My shouts were so authoritative, my gestures so arresting, that I commanded the situation like a lion-tamer, and the dogs finally slunk away.

Looking back, I think I acted less in anger than from a realization that I was on my own, that if anybody was going to help me at that moment, it had to be myself.

Life seems to be a series of crises that have to be faced. In summoning strength to face them, though, I once fooled myself into an exaggerated regard of my own importance. I felt very independent. I was only distantly aware of other people. I worked hard and was "successful." In the theater, I was brought up in the tradition of service. The audience pays its money and you are expected to give your best performance—both on and off the stage. So I served on committees, and made speeches, and backed causes. But somehow the *meaning* of things escaped me.

When my daughter died of polio, everybody stretched out a hand to help me, but at first I couldn't seem to bear the touch of anything, even the love of friends; no support seemed strong enough.

While Mary was still sick, I used to go early in the morning to a little church near the hospital to pray. There the working people came quietly to worship. I had been careless with my religion. I had rather cut God out of my life, and I didn't have the nerve at the time to ask Him to make my daughter well—I only asked Him to help me understand, to let me come in and reach Him, and I kept looking for a revelation, but nothing happened.

And then, much later, I discovered that it *had* happened, right there in the church. I could recall, vividly, one by one, the people I had seen there—the solemn laborers with tired looks, the old women with gnarled hands. Life had knocked them around, but for a brief moment they were being refreshed by an ennobling experience. It seemed as they prayed their worn faces lighted up and they became the very vessels of God. Here was my revelation. Suddenly I realized I was one of them. In my need I gained strength from the knowledge that they too had needs, and I felt an interdependence with them. I was learning the meaning of "Love thy neighbor . . ."

Truths as old and simple as this began to light up for me like the faces of the men and women in the little church. When I read the Bible now, I take the teachings of men like Jesus and David and St. Paul as the helpful advice of trusted friends about how to live. They understand that life is full of complications, and often heavy blows, and they are showing me the wisest way through it. I must help myself, yes, but I am not such a self-contained unit that I can live aloof, unto myself. That was the meaning that had been missing before: the realization that I was a living part of God's world of people.

Known as the First Lady of American Theater, HELEN HAYES *was a star of Broadway, movies, and television. She received three Tony Awards in her sixty years onstage. Her movies ranged from* The Sin of Madelon Claudet *(1931) to* Airport *(1970), both of which garnered her Academy Awards.*

Our Noble, Essential Decency

Robert A. Heinlein,
as featured in the 1950s series

I AM NOT GOING TO TALK ABOUT RELIGIOUS BELIEFS but about matters so obvious that it has gone out of style to mention them. I believe in my neighbors. I know their faults, and I know that their virtues far outweigh their faults.

Take Father Michael, down our road a piece. I'm not of his creed, but I know that goodness and charity and loving kindness shine in his daily actions. I believe in Father Mike. If I'm in trouble, I'll go to him. My next-door neighbor's a veterinary doctor. Doc will get out of bed after a hard day to help a stray cat—no fee, no prospect of a fee. I believe in Doc.

I believe in my townspeople. You can knock on any door in our town, say, "I'm hungry," and you'll be fed. Our town is no exception. I've found the same ready charity everywhere. For the one who says, "The heck with you, I've got mine," there are a hundred, a thousand, who will say, "Sure pal, sit down." I know that despite all warnings against hitchhikers, I can step to the highway, thumb for a ride, and in a few minutes a car or a truck will stop and someone will say, "Climb in, Mack. How far you going?"

I believe in my fellow citizens. Our headlines are splashed with crime. Yet for every criminal, there are ten thousand honest, decent, kindly men. If it were not so, no child would live to grow up. Business could not go on from day to day. Decency is not news. It is buried in the obituaries, but it is a force stronger than crime.

I believe in the patient gallantry of nurses, in the tedious sacrifices of teachers. I believe in the unseen and unending fight against desperate odds that goes on quietly in almost every home in the land. I believe in the honest craft of workmen. Take a look around you. There never were enough bosses to check up on all that work. From Independence Hall to the Grand Coulee Dam, these things were built level and square by craftsmen who were honest in their bones.

I believe that almost all politicians are honest. For every bribed alderman, there are hundreds of politicians—low paid or not paid at all—doing their level best without thanks or glory to make our system work. If this were not true, we would never have gotten past the thirteen colonies.

I believe in Rodger Young. You and I are free today because of endless unnamed heroes from Valley Forge to the Yalu River. I believe in—I am proud to belong to—the United States. Despite shortcomings—from lynchings, to bad faith in high places—our nation has had the most decent and kindly internal practices and foreign policies to be found anywhere in history.

And finally, I believe in my whole race—yellow, white, black, red, brown—in the honesty, courage, intelligence, durability, and *goodness* of the overwhelming majority of my brothers and sisters everywhere on this planet. I am proud to be a human being. I believe that we have come this far by the skin of our teeth—that we always make it just for the skin of our teeth—but that we will always make it, survive, endure.

I believe that this hairless embryo with the aching oversized braincase and the opposable thumb—this animal barely up from the apes—will endure, will endure longer than his home planet, will spread out to the other planets—to the stars and beyond—carrying with him his honesty, his insatiable curiosity, his unlimited courage, and his noble essential decency. This I believe with all my heart.

This I Believe

> Robert A. Heinlein won four Hugo Awards during his fifty-year career as a science fiction writer. Born and raised in Missouri, he graduated from the U.S. Naval Academy in 1929 and did aeronautical engineering for the Navy during World War II. Heinlein's books include Starship Troopers and Stranger in a Strange Land.

A New Birth of Freedom

Maximilian Hodder,
as featured in the 1950s series

To state clearly and honestly one's beliefs in a few hundred words is a large order in any man's language, particularly so if one has been a victim of a number of very personal tragedies.

Ever since my adolescent mind began to comprehend the complexities of our daily life, I looked upon a human being as a personification of that great unknown with a very specific mission on earth to fulfill. I looked for perfection, for love, and understanding. I believed in human beings.

Then one day from the world of a carefree, happy life of a young, up-and-coming writer/director in prewar Poland,

I was thrown into the Nazis' and, later, Communists' world of hatred, tyranny, murder, and destruction. Human being ceased to be what I believed it was destined for, and I became the raw material for a soap factory—an implement in a five-year plan, or a guinea pig in a biological laboratory. I lost my country and my family, and my belief in human beings was crushed mercilessly. I became bitter and cynical.

Then came the third and, to me perhaps, the most significant period of my life so far: here in America. From the moment the immigration officer at La Guardia Airport shook my hand and wished me good luck, I again began to see the sunnier side of life. I have made true friends and they have proven themselves when I needed them most. Food and clothing for victims of floods; a group of GIs adopting an orphan and sending him to school; neighbors building a new home for a victim of fire; Community Chest, Cancer Fund, Salvation Army, Alcoholics Anonymous, and a thousand other such acts or associations, all voluntary, collective or individual, left an indelible mark on me. It gave me a new lease on life. I again believe in mankind.

I now remember not only the days when people were chased from houses of worship with guns, but also those poor Russians who traded for food their most treasured possessions but kept the holy icons. I now think not only of those who killed, but also of the kind Russian peasants who met our convoy to Siberia and, in spite of guys who chased them away, tried to share with us corned beef, a piece of bread, perhaps their last one. I also think of those gun-starved wretches who after years of unendurable exploitation in forced labor camps, still had enough humanness left in them to sing or even joke occasionally.

I now again believe there is more good than evil; more of those who create, or wish to create, than those who destroy; more of those who love than those who hate. I firmly believe in an inalienable right of the individual to live the life of his choice, his right to work or rest, smile or cry, succeed or fail, pray or play. The great Polish poet Adam Mickiewicz said, "The nectar of life is sweet only when shared with others." I therefore also believe that it is my duty to contribute, in whatever way I can, to the present struggle to bring hope to those still oppressed, so that, as a great American once said, "They also may, under God, have a new birth of freedom."

Director MAXIMILIAN HODDER *worked in the movie industries of Eastern Europe. While serving in the Polish Army during World War II, he was captured by the Soviets but managed to escape and went on to join the Royal Air Force. Hodder came to the United States in 1949 to work in Hollywood.*

The Benefits of Restlessness and Jagged Edges

Kay Redfield Jamison

I BELIEVE THAT CURIOSITY, WONDER, AND PASSION are defining qualities of imaginative minds and great teachers; that restlessness and discontent are vital things; and that intense experience and suffering instruct us in ways less intense emotions can never do. I believe, in short, we are equally beholden to heart and mind, and that those who have particularly passionate temperaments and questioning minds leave the world a different place for their having been there. It is important to value intellect and discipline, of course, but it is also important to recognize the power of irrationality, enthusiasm, and vast energy. Intensity has its costs, of course—in pain, in hastily and poorly reckoned plans, in impetuousness—but it has its advantages as well.

Like millions of Americans, I was dealt a hand of intense emotions and volatile moods. I have had manic-depressive illness, also known as bipolar disorder, since I was eighteen years old. It is an illness that ensures that those who have it will experience a frightening, chaotic, and emotional ride. It is not a gentle or easy disease. And, yet, from it I have come to see how important a certain restlessness and discontent can be in one's life; how important the jagged edges and pain can be in determining the course and force of one's life.

I have often longed for peace and tranquility—looked into the lives of others and envied a kind of calmness—and yet I don't know if this tranquility is what I truly would have wished for myself. One is, after all, only really acquainted with one's own temperament and way of going through life. It is best to acknowledge this, to accept it, and to admire the diversity of temperaments Nature has dealt us.

An intense temperament has convinced me to teach not only from books, but from what I have learned from experience. So I try to impress upon young doctors and graduate students that tumultuousness, if coupled to discipline and a cool mind, is not such a bad sort of thing. That unless one wants to live a stunningly boring life, one ought to be on good terms with one's darker side and one's darker energies. And, above all, that one should learn from turmoil and pain, share one's joy with those less joyful, and encourage passion when it seems likely to promote the common good.

Knowledge is marvelous, but wisdom is even better.

Kay Redfield Jamison is a professor of psychiatry at the Johns Hopkins School of Medicine. She has written a number of books, including An Unquiet Mind *and* Exuberance: The Passion for Life. *She was honored with a prestigious MacArthur Fellowship in 2001.*

There Is No God

Penn Jillette

I BELIEVE THAT THERE IS NO GOD. I'm beyond Atheism. Atheism is not believing in god. Not believing in god is easy, you can't prove a negative, so there's no work to do. You can't prove that there isn't an elephant inside the trunk of my car. You sure? How about now? Maybe he was just hiding before. Check again. Did I mention that my personal heartfelt definition of the word "elephant" includes mystery, order, goodness, love, and a spare tire?

So, anyone with a love for truth outside of herself has to start with no belief in god and then look for evidence of god. She needs to search for some objective evidence of a supernatural power. All the people I write e-mails to often are still stuck at this searching stage. The Atheism part is easy.

But, this "This I Believe" thing seems to demand something more personal, some leap of faith that helps one see life's big picture, some rules to live by. So, I'm saying, "This I believe—I believe there is no god."

Having taken that step, it informs every moment of my life. I'm not greedy. I have love, blue skies, rainbows, and Hallmark cards, and that has to be enough. It has to be enough, but it's everything in the world, and everything in the world is plenty for me. It seems just rude to beg the invisible for more. Just the love of my family that raised me and the family I'm raising now is enough that I don't need heaven. I won the huge genetic lottery, and I get joy every day.

Believing there's no god means I can't really be forgiven except by kindness and faulty memories. That's good; it makes me want to be more thoughtful. I have to try to treat people right the first time around.

Believing there's no god stops me from being solipsistic. I can read ideas from all different people from all different cultures. Without god, we can agree on reality, and I can keep learning where I'm wrong. We can all keep adjusting, so we can really communicate. I don't travel in circles where people say, "I have faith, I believe this in my heart, and nothing you can say or do can shake my faith." That's just a long-winded religious way to say, "shut up," or another two words that the FCC likes less. But, all obscenity is less insulting than, "How I was brought up and my imaginary friend means more to me than anything you can ever say or do." So, believing there is no god lets me be proven wrong and that's always fun. It means I'm learning something.

Believing there is no god means the suffering I've seen in my family, and indeed all the suffering in the world, isn't caused by an omniscient, omnipresent, omnipotent force that isn't bothered to help or is just testing us, but rather something we all may be able to help others with in the future. No god means the possibility of less suffering in the future.

Believing there is no god gives me more room for belief in family, people, love, truth, beauty, sex, Jell-O, and all the other things I can prove and that make this life the best life I will ever have.

PENN JILLETTE *is the taller, louder half of the magic and comedy act Penn and Teller. He is a research fellow at the Cato Institute and has lectured at Oxford and MIT. Penn has coauthored three bestselling books and was executive producer of the documentary film* The Aristocrats.

A Duty to Heal

Pius Kamau

Growing up in the grinding poverty of colonial Africa, America was my shining hope. Martin Luther King's nonviolent political struggle made freedom and equality sound like achievable goals. America's ideals filled my head. Someday, I promised myself, I would walk on America's streets.

But, as soon as I set foot in America's hospitals, reality—and racism—quickly intruded on the ideals. My color and accent set me apart. But in a hospital I am neither black nor white. I'm a doctor. I believe every patient that I touch deserves the same care and concern from me.

In 1999, I was on-call when a nineteen-year-old patient

was brought into the hospital. He was coughing up blood after a car accident. He was a white supremacist, an American Nazi with a swastika tattooed on his chest.

The nurses told me he would not let me touch him. When I came close to him, he spat on me. In that moment, I wanted no part of him, either, but no other physician would take him on. I realized I had to minister to him as best as I could.

I talked to him, but he refused to look at me or acknowledge me. He would only speak through the white nurses. Only they could check his body for injury. Only they could touch his tattooed chest.

As it turned out, he was not badly hurt. We parted strangers.

I still wonder: Was there more I could have done to make our encounter different or better? Could I have approached him differently? Could I have tried harder to win his trust?

I can only guess his thoughts about me, or the beliefs he lived by. His racism, I think, had little to do with me, personally. And, I want to think it had little to do with America, with the faith of Martin Luther King and other great men whose words I heard back in Africa, and who made me believe in this nation's ideals of equality and freedom.

My hands—my black hands—have saved many lives. I believe in my duty to heal. I believe all patients, all human beings, are equal, and that I must try to care for everyone, even those who would rather die than consider me their equal.

Before coming to the United States in 1971, PIUS KAMAU *studied medicine in his native Kenya as well as in Spain and England. In addition to being a thoracic and general surgeon, he writes a column on African issues for the* Denver Post. *Kamau is organizing medical volunteers to work with him in Sudan.*

Living Life with "Grace and Elegant Treeness"

Ruth Kamps

Sitting on our small deck, knitting and resting old legs, I am entertained by my spiritual sister, an equally old pine tree. She is very tall, probably forty feet or so, and is at least as old as I am. She leans a bit; so do I. In her care are many birds that I watch with pleasure. They love and fight and nest in the tree. At Christmastime, pairs of cardinals decorate her limbs.

She is still green, covering lots of old brown branches, like my gray hair covering the black. We both soak in the sun and air and are trying our best to live lightly in our worlds. One day in the not-too-distant future she will fall and fertilize the earth, as I will do. It's a consoling thought.

We have children and grandchildren to give us the continuation of life. A bit of the divine in the tree and me. Yes, that's close to what I believe.

My husband, John, and I moved to the country from a suburb and a traditional church nearly forty years ago. Our property is in the Kettle Moraine of Wisconsin. It slopes sharply down to a stream that glows red with the setting sun. When my parents came to visit after our move, my father said I would not be happy here; I was a city girl. He was right in the beginning. I was too busy, too poor, and very lonely.

When my mother died, I was pregnant and needed her. I went to the church to be quiet and cry. The church was locked and the priest was standing outside. He knew me but did not unlock the church. I don't know why, but it was a nail in the coffin of my traditional beliefs. We had nine family-related deaths in one year. I learned to watch the red setting sun and was calmed, soothed, and grateful, at least for a moment. I began to like digging in the dirt instead of cursing each weed. Cutting the evil buckthorn in the woods became a spiritual experience. I started to spend Sunday morning in the woods. Was I losing long-held beliefs or simply changing them?

I found an answer while traveling. I was asked if I were religious, while standing at the rail of a cruise ship with a fellow traveler on the Yangtze River. I said I was not but that I was spiritual. I was asked to explain. I talked about my sister tree. A cab driver in Rome said that one must live in a place a long time to appreciate its beauty. Is forty years enough? Taking frequent trips to the brashness of Chicago to see children and grandchildren always energized me. It still does, but I miss the woods.

I have lost most of my traditional heaven-and-hell beliefs, finding them used conveniently by good people. There is a bit of the divine in the trees and the creatures who reside there. A little wren attacks a large, red-bellied woodpecker who is pecking too close to his nest. I am filled with admiration. The transition is complete.

There are those who want to give my life more importance than the tree, but I don't believe them. They think there is a special place for me somewhere for eternity, but I don't believe them. I believe my tree and all other living things believe and feel in their particular living ways. I want to work on being as good a human as I am able, just as my tree does her job with grace and elegant treeness.

RUTH KAMPS *is a retired elementary schoolteacher in rural Wisconsin. In 1967, she and her husband moved into his childhood home. When not admiring her pine tree from her deck or out her kitchen window, Kamps is an avid knitter and reader.*

The Light of a Brighter Day

HELEN KELLER,
AS FEATURED IN THE 1950S SERIES

I CHOOSE FOR MY SUBJECT, faith wrought into life apart from creed or dogma. By faith, I mean a vision of good one cherishes and enthusiasm that pushes one to seek its fulfillment, regardless of obstacles. Faith is a dynamic power that breaks the chain of routine, and gives a new, fine turn to old commonplaces. Faith reinvigorates the will, enriches the affections, and awakens a sense of creativeness. Active faith knows no fear, and it is a safeguard to me against cynicism and despair.

After all, faith is not one thing or two or three things. It is an indivisible totality of beliefs that inspire me: belief in

God as infinite goodwill and all-seeing Wisdom, whose everlasting arms sustain me walking on the sea of life. Trust in my fellow men, wonder at their fundamental goodness, and confidence that after this night of sorrow and oppression, they will rise up strong and beautiful in the glory of morning. Reverence for the beauty and preciousness of the earth, and a sense of responsibility to do what I can to make it a habitation of health and plenty for all men. Faith in immortality because it renders less bitter the separation from those I have loved and lost, and because it will free me from unnatural limitations, and unfold still more faculties I have in joyous activity.

Even if my vital spark should be blown out, I believe that I should behave with courageous dignity in the presence of fate and strive to be a worthy companion of the beautiful, the good, and the true. But fate has its master in the faith of those who surmount it, and limitation has its limits for those who, though disillusioned, live greatly.

It was a terrible blow to my faith when I learned that millions of my fellow creatures must labor all their days for food and shelter, bear the most crushing burdens, and die without having known the joy of living. My security vanished forever, and I have never regained the radiant belief of my young years that earth is a happy home and hearth for the majority of mankind. But faith is a state of mind. The believer is not soon disheartened. If he is turned out of his shelter, he builds up a house that the winds of the earth cannot destroy.

When I think of the suffering and famine, and the continued slaughter of men, my spirit bleeds. But the thought comes to me that, like the little deaf, dumb, and blind child I once was, mankind is growing out of the darkness of ignorance and hate into the light of a brighter day.

As an infant, HELEN KELLER *was struck by a fever that left her deaf and blind. But with the guidance of her teacher, Anne Sullivan, she learned to communicate through the eyes and ears of others. After graduating from Radcliffe College, Keller became a renowned author, activist, and lecturer.*

The Bright Lights of Freedom

Harold Hongju Koh

I BELIEVE THAT FREEDOM IS CONTAGIOUS.

My parents were born in South Korea and came here more than fifty years ago. They came for the education and for the freedom. They grew up under Japanese colonial rule, forbidden to speak Korean or even to use their Korean names. When their country was divided after World War II, my mother and her family were trapped in North Korea. In desperation, they hiked for days to the border to be picked up, and were brought back to Seoul. But even there, they lived under dictatorship. For less than a year in the 1960s, Korea enjoyed democracy, and my father joined the diplomatic corps. But one day, tanks rolled and a coup d'état toppled the government, leaving us to grow up in America.

My father savored freedom like he savored fresh air. He loved the freedom to follow his passions: for John F. Kennedy, for Fred Astaire, for Ted Williams. Driving down the road, he would turn and exclaim: "This is a great, great country. Here, we can do what we want."

During the summer that President Nixon resigned, I was visiting Seoul. Someone tried to assassinate Korea's president and he declared martial law. I called my father and marveled that Korea had never enjoyed a peaceful transition of government. Meanwhile the world's most powerful government had just changed hands without anyone firing a shot. He said, "Now you see the difference: In a democracy, if you are president, then the troops obey you. In a dictatorship, if the troops obey you, then you are president."

And so I studied law, became a law professor and dean, and eventually a human rights official for the State Department. I traveled to scores of countries. Everywhere I went—Haiti, Indonesia, China, Sierra Leone, Kosovo—I saw in the eyes of thousands the same fire for freedom I had first seen in my father's eyes. Once an Asian dictator told us to stop imposing our Western values on his people. He said, "We Asians don't feel the same way as Americans do about human rights." I pointed to my own face and told him he was wrong.

As my time in government ended, I traveled to North Korea. In the eyes of everyone—children, workers, government officials—I saw the lifeless, unfocused stares I had first read about in Orwell's *1984*. I saw people whose aspirations had been crushed by a government that would not provide for their most basic needs. As we flew out of a darkened Pyongyang, I looked down to see where my mother had crossed the border so many years ago. As we approached Seoul, suddenly the landscape glowed with millions of lights. I realized that the only differences between the bright futures to the South and the dark futures of the North were the governments that ruled them.

That is why I believe in the bright lights of freedom.

HAROLD HONGJU KOH *is dean of Yale Law School, where he teaches human rights and international law. From 1998 to 2001, he served as assistant secretary of state for Democracy, Human Rights, and Labor. Born in Boston, Koh is a lifelong Red Sox fan.*

The Power of Love to Transform and Heal

JACKIE LANTRY

I BELIEVE IN THE INGREDIENTS OF LOVE, the elements from which it is made. I believe in love's humble, practical components and their combined power.

We adopted Luke four years ago. The people from the orphanage dropped him off at our hotel room without even saying good-bye. He was nearly six years old, only twenty-eight pounds, and his face was crisscrossed with scars. Clearly, he was terrified. "What are his favorite things?" I yelled. "Noodles," they replied as the elevator door shut.

Luke kicked and screamed. I stood between him and the door to keep him from bolting. His cries were anguished, animal-like. He had never seen a mirror and tried to escape by running through one. I wound my arms around him so he could not hit or kick. After an hour and a half he finally fell asleep, exhausted. I called room service. They delivered every noodle dish on the menu. Luke woke up, looked at me, and started sobbing again. I handed him chopsticks and pointed at the food. He stopped crying and started to eat. He ate until I was sure he would be sick.

That night we went for a walk. Delighted at the moon, he pantomimed, "What is it?" I said, "The moon, it's the moon." He reached up and tried to touch it. He cried again when I tried to give him a bath until I started to play with the water. By the end of his bath the room was soaked and he was giggling. I lotioned him up, powdered him down, and clothed him in soft pj's. We read the book *One Yellow Lion*. He loved looking at the colorful pictures and turning the pages. By the end of the night he was saying "one yellow lion."

The next day we met orphanage officials to do paperwork. Luke was on my lap as they filed into the room. He looked at them and wrapped my arms tightly around his waist.

He was a sad, shy boy for a long time after those first days. He cried easily and withdrew at the slightest provocation. He hid food in his pillowcase and foraged in garbage cans. I wondered then if he would ever get over the wounds of neglect that the orphanage had beaten into him.

It has been four years. Luke is a smart, funny, happy fourth grader. He is loaded with charm and is a natural athlete. His teachers say he is well-behaved and works very hard. Our neighbor says she has never seen a happier kid.

When I think back, I am amazed at what transformed this abused, terrified little creature. It was not therapy, counselors, or medications. It did not cost money or require connections or great privilege. It was love: just simple, plain, easy to give. Love is primal. It is comprised of compassion, care, security, and a leap of faith. I believe in the power of love to transform. I believe in the power of love to heal.

JACKIE LANTRY *is a part-time hospital clerk in Rehoboth, Massachusetts. She and her husband have adopted two girls and two boys from China. When Jackie asked her children what they believed in, they said "family."*

The Power of Mysteries

Alan Lightman

I BELIEVE IN THE POWER OF THE UNKNOWN. I believe that a sense of the unknown propels us in all of our creative activities, from science to art.

When I was a child, after bedtime I would often get out of my bed in my pajamas, go to the window, and stare at the stars. I had so many questions. How far away were those tiny points of light? Did space go on forever and ever, or was there some end to space, some giant edge. And if so, what lay beyond the edge?

Another of my childhood questions: Did time go on forever? I looked at pictures of my parents and grandparents and tried to imagine their parents, and so on, back through the generations, back and back through time. Looking out of my bedroom window into the vastness of space, time seemed to stretch forward and backward without end, engulfing me, engulfing my parents and great-grandparents, engulfing the entire history of earth. Does time go on forever? Or is there some beginning of time? And if so, what came before?

When I grew up, I became a professional astrophysicist. Although I never answered any of these questions, they continued to challenge me, to haunt me, to drive me in my scientific research, to cause me to live on tuna fish and no sleep for days at a time while I was obsessed with a science problem. These same questions, and questions like them, challenge and haunt the leading scientists of today.

Einstein once wrote, "The most beautiful experience we can have is the mysterious. It is the fundamental emotion which stands at the cradle of true art and true science." What did Einstein mean by "the mysterious"? I don't think he meant that science is full of unpredictable or unknowable or supernatural forces. I think that he meant a sense of awe, a sense that there are things larger than us, that we don't have all the answers at this moment. A sense that we can stand right at the boundary between known and unknown and gaze into that cavern and be exhilarated rather than frightened.

Scientists are happy, of course, when they find answers to questions. But scientists are also happy when they become stuck, when they discover interesting questions that they can't answer. Because that is when their imaginations and creativity are set on fire. That is when the greatest progress occurs.

One of the Holy Grails in physics is to find the so-called Theory of Everything, the final theory that will encompass all the fundamental laws of nature. I, for one, hope that we never find that final theory. I hope that there are always things that we don't know—about the physical world as well as about ourselves. I believe in the creative power of the unknown. I believe in the exhilaration of standing at the boundary between the known and the unknown. I believe in the unanswered questions of children.

ALAN LIGHTMAN *is an astrophysicist and novelist teaching at the Massachusetts Institute of Technology. He is the author of* Einstein's Dreams *and* A Sense of the Mysterious: Science and the Human Spirit. *Lightman and his wife, Jean, started the Harpswell Foundation to help disadvantaged students in Cambodia obtain an education.*

Life Grows in the Soil of Time

THOMAS MANN,
AS FEATURED IN THE 1950S SERIES

WHAT I BELIEVE, WHAT I VALUE MOST, is transitoriness.

But is not transitoriness—the perishableness of life—something very sad? No! It is the very soul of existence. It imparts value, dignity, interest to life. Transitoriness creates *time*—and "time is the essence." Potentially at least, time is the supreme, most useful gift.

Time is related to—yes, identical with—everything creative and active, with every progress toward a higher goal.

Without transitoriness, without beginning or end, birth or death, there is no time, either. Timelessness—in the sense of time never ending, never beginning—is a stagnant nothing. It is absolutely uninteresting.

Life is possessed by tremendous tenacity. Even so, its presence remains conditional, and as it had a beginning, so it will have an end. I believe that life, just for this reason, is exceedingly enhanced in value, in charm.

One of the most important characteristics distinguishing man from all other forms of nature is his knowledge of transitoriness, of beginning and end, and therefore of the gift of time.

In man, transitory life attains its peak of animation, of soul power, so to speak. This does not mean man alone would have a soul. Soul quality pervades all beings. But man's soul is most awake in his knowledge of the interchangeability of the terms "existence" and "transitoriness."

To man, time is given like a piece of land, as it were, entrusted to him for faithful tilling; a space in which to strive incessantly, achieve self-realization, move onward and upward. Yes, with the aid of time, man becomes capable of wresting the immortal from the mortal.

Deep down, I believe—and deem such belief natural to every human soul—that in the universe, prime significance must be attributed to this earth of ours. Deep down, I believe that creation of the universe out of nothingness and that of life out of inorganic state ultimately aimed at the creation of man. I believe that man is meant as a great experiment whose possible failure by man's own guilt would be paramount to the failure of creation itself.

Whether this belief be true or not, man would be well-advised if he behaved as though it were.

> *Nobel Prize–winning author* THOMAS MANN *was noted for his examination and critique of the European and German soul in the first half of the twentieth century. Known for their insight into the psychology of the artist, his major works include* Death in Venice, The Magic Mountain, *and* Doctor Faustus.

Why I Close My Restaurant

George Mardikian,
as featured in the 1950s series

Every Christmas eve, I close my restaurant to the public. My wife and I become the hired help to serve our employees. We try to give them the finest Christmas repast. This exchange of roles is symbolic. This is an ancient Armenian custom we have introduced into our American life.

Each national group has brought something of its heritage in the form of thousands of different customs, which have become integral parts of life in this country. I believe that true humility is a basic need of mankind today. Why do I believe this? Aside from the fact that Jesus Christ taught it, my own experience seems to me a living testimony of its truth.

As a young man in my native Armenia, I was organizing boy scout troops when the Turks and the Russians invaded the Republic of Armenia. I was captured and thrown into prison. I nearly starved to death in this time of crisis. An older and wiser inmate said to me, "Don't lose hope." He was right, for some American friends in the Near East Relief helped me to escape. They used the ruse of telling my captors that I was an American. I became an American before I *became* an American.

Eventually, I was able to work my way to the United States. Here I was, a humble immigrant boy crossing the Atlantic to a country that seemed to answer all my prayers for happiness and freedom. My feelings when I first saw the Statue of Liberty cannot be described. Even today, when I pass it on my frequent trips to Europe, a feeling—something like reverence—comes over me.

When I entered the shower baths at Ellis Island, I found plenty of soap and water. I used them freely because it seemed to me that I was washing away all the hatreds and prejudices of the old world. As I stepped out of the shower and came face to face with a guard in uniform, he actually *smiled* at me. The smile of a stranger may seem to be a fleeting, insignificant moment to others, but I remember it vividly because it set the mood for my new life. It was perhaps an omen of the joy and friendship I was to find about me.

When I first arrived, I spoke very little English and had practically no money. But I did have enthusiasm, the will to work, and bright hopes for a new life ahead. I got on the westbound train for San Francisco. Everywhere I went strangers were willing to help, and I felt very humble.

This wonderful land has been good to me. It has given me friends by the hundreds in all walks of life. I believe that in this society, where love and mutual respect are fostered and encouraged, I must do more than contribute my share toward the material and the spiritual well-being of all. I believe that friendship, which grows out of love and true humility, is the most important thing in life.

GEORGE MARDIKIAN's *first job in America was washing dishes in a San Francisco cafeteria; he eventually bought the place and built it into a renowned restaurant. For his work to improve food service for combat troops in Korea, Mardikian was awarded the Medal of Freedom, the highest civilian award an American can receive.*

The Virtues of the Quiet Hero

John McCain

I BELIEVE IN HONOR, FAITH, AND SERVICE—to one's country and to mankind. It's a lesson I learned from my family, from the men with whom I served in Vietnam, and from my fellow Americans.

Take William B. Ravnel. He was in Patton's tank corps that went across Europe. I knew him, though, as an English teacher and football coach in my school. He could make Shakespeare come alive, and he had incredible leadership talents that made me idolize him. What he taught me more than anything else was to strictly adhere to our school's honor code. If we stuck to those standards of integrity and honor, then we could be proud of ourselves. We could serve causes greater than our own self-interest.

Years later, I saw an example of honor in the most surprising of places. As a scared American prisoner of war in Vietnam, I was tied in torture ropes by my tormentors and left alone in an empty room to suffer through the night. Later in the evening, a guard I had never spoken to entered the room and silently loosened the ropes to relieve my suffering. Just before morning, that same guard came back and retightened the ropes before his less humanitarian comrades returned. He never said a word to me. Some months later on a Christmas morning, as I stood alone in the prison courtyard, that same guard walked up to me and stood next to me for a few moments. Then, with his sandal, the guard drew a cross in the dirt. We stood wordlessly there for a minute or two, venerating the cross, until the guard rubbed it out and walked away.

To me, that was faith: a faith that unites and never divides, a faith that bridges unbridgeable gaps in humanity. It is the faith that we are all equal and endowed by our Creator with inalienable rights to life, liberty, and the pursuit of happiness. It is a faith I would die to defend.

My determination to act with honor and integrity impels me to work in service to my country. I have believed that the means to real happiness and the true worth of a person is measured by how faithfully we serve a cause greater than our self-interest. In America, we celebrate the virtues of the quiet hero—the modest man who does his duty without complaint or expectation of praise; the man who listens closely for the call of his country, and when she calls, he answers without reservation, not for fame or reward, but for love.

I have been an imperfect servant of my country, and my mistakes rightly humble me. I have tried to live by these principles of honor, faith, and service because I want my children to live by them as well. I hope to be a good example to them so that when their generation takes our place, they will make better decisions and continue to pave the path toward righteousness and freedom.

JOHN MCCAIN *is the son and grandson of U.S. Navy admirals. After graduating from Annapolis as a naval aviator, McCain was shot down over North Vietnam and spent five years as a prisoner of war. He has been a U.S. senator from Arizona since 1986 and ran for president in 2000.*

The Joy and Enthusiasm of Reading

Rick Moody

I BELIEVE IN THE ABSOLUTE AND UNLIMITED liberty of reading. I believe in wandering through the stacks and picking out the first thing that strikes me. I believe in choosing books based on the dust jacket. I believe in reading books because others dislike them or find them dangerous. I believe in choosing the hardest book imaginable. I believe in reading up on what others have to say about this difficult book, and then making up my own mind.

Part of this has to do with Mr. Buxton, who taught me Shakespeare in tenth grade. We were reading *Macbeth*. Mr. Buxton, who probably had better things to do, nonetheless agreed to meet one night to go over the text line by line. The first thing he did was point out the repetition of motifs—for example, the reversals of things ("fair is foul and foul is fair"). Then there was the unsexing of Lady Macbeth and the association in the play of masculinity with violence.

What Mr. Buxton didn't tell me was what the play *meant.* He left the conclusions to me. The situation was much the same with my religious studies teacher in eleventh grade, Mr. Flanders, who encouraged me to have my own relationship with the Gospels, and perhaps he quoted Jesus of Nazareth in the process. "Therefore speak I to them in parables: Because they seeing, see not; and hearing they hear not, neither do they understand."

High school was followed by college, where I read Umberto Eco's *Role of the Reader,* in which it is said that the reader completes the text, that the text is never finished until it meets this voracious and engaged reader. The open texts, Eco calls them. In college, I read some of the great Europeans and Latin Americans: Borges and Kafka, Genet and Beckett, Artaud, Proust—open texts all. I may not have known *why* Kafka's *Metamorphosis* is about a guy who turns into a bug, but I knew that some said cockroach, and others, European dung beetle.

There are those critics, of course, who insist that there are right ways and wrong ways to read every book. No doubt they arrived at these beliefs through their own adventures in the stacks. And these are important questions for philosophers of every stripe. And yet I know only what joy and enthusiasm about reading have taught me, in bookstores new and used.

I believe there is not now and never will be an authority who can tell me how to interpret, how to read, how to find the pearl of literary meaning in all cases. Nietzsche says, "Supposing truth is a woman—what then?" Supposing the truth is not hard, fast, masculine, simple, direct? You could spend a lifetime thinking about this sentence, and making it your own. In just this way, I believe in the freedom to see literature, history, truth, unfolding ahead of me like a book whose spine has just now been cracked.

RICK MOODY *is a writer of short stories and novels, many of which explore disintegrating family bonds in suburban America. He lives on Long Island and cofounded the Young Lions Book Award at the New York Public Library. In his memoir,* The Black Veil, *Moody identifies reading as key to developing an identity.*

There Is Such a Thing as Truth

Errol Morris

I BELIEVE IN TRUTH. And in the pursuit of truth.

When I was ten years old, I asked a neighborhood kid who was older than me, "Which city is further west: Reno, Nevada, or Los Angeles?" The correct answer is Reno, Nevada. But he was convinced it was the other way around.

He was so convinced that Los Angeles was west of Reno that he was willing to bet me two bucks. So I went into the house to get my Rand McNally Atlas. The kid looked at the atlas and said, "This map is drawn funny." It wasn't. Was his argument that the map didn't preserve east, west, north, and south? What kind of map would that be?

I showed him if you trace down the 120-degree west line of longitude—which runs almost directly through Reno, Nevada—you end up in the Pacific Ocean, somewhere west of Los Angeles.

He replied, "Lines of longitude don't cross the ocean."

What? I told him that the lines of longitude were there to indicate how far west or east some location was, regardless of whether it was on land or on sea.

There was one insurmountable problem, however. He was bigger than me.

I drew a number of conclusions from this story. There is such a thing as truth, but we often have a vested interest in ignoring it or outright denying it. Also, it's not just thinking something that makes it true. Truth is not relative. It's not subjective. It may be elusive or hidden. People may wish to disregard it. But there is such a thing as truth and the pursuit of truth: trying to figure out what has really happened, trying to figure out how things really are.

Almost fifteen years ago, I stumbled on a story about an innocent man, a man who had been sentenced to die in the Huntsville, Texas, electric chair. And through hard work, luck, and a certain amount of pathological obsession, I was able to make the movie *The Thin Blue Line* and help get him out of prison.

What kept me going was the belief that there had to be

answers to the questions "Did he do it?," "Was he guilty or innocent?," "If he didn't do it, who did?" and that I could find an answer to these questions through investigating.

It's not that we find truth with a big "T." We investigate and sometimes we find things out and sometimes we don't. There's no way to know in advance. It's just that we have to proceed as though there are answers to questions. We must proceed as though, in principle, we can find things out—even if we can't. The alternative is unacceptable.

I will never know whether the neighborhood kid really didn't understand the logic of my argument about Reno, Nevada. Or whether he understood it completely and just didn't want to admit it. Or whether he understood it and just didn't want to pay up. I'll never know.

All I know is I never got my two dollars.

ERROL MORRIS *is an Academy Award–winning documentary filmmaker whose works include* The Thin Blue Line *and* The Fog of War: Eleven Lessons from the Life of Robert S. McNamara. *He is also the director of critically acclaimed television programs and commercials. Early in his life, Morris worked as a private detective.*

The Rule of Law

Michael Mullane

For the most part, my personal belief—or yours, for that matter—is not particularly important to society. On the other hand, our beliefs about *some* things are very important. These are things subject to the Tinkerbell effect—that is, they *exist* only so long as we believe in them. One of these is the rule of law. When you get right down to it, the rule of law only exists because enough of us believe in it and insist that everyone, even the nonbelievers, behave as if it exists. The minute enough of us stop believing, stop insisting that the law protect us all, and that every single one of us is accountable to the law—in that moment, the rule of law will be gone.

So I cling to my belief in the rule of law. It is probably the single greatest achievement of our society. It is our bulwark against both mob rule and the overweening power of the modern state. It is the rule of law that governs us, that protects each one of us when we stand alone against those who disagree with us, or fear us, or do not like us because we are different. It is the strongbox that keeps all our other values safe.

The law is wonderfully strong and terribly fragile. In times of crisis and threat, there is a temptation to stop believing in the rule of law—a temptation to think that it weakens rather than protects us. We have succumbed to this temptation more than once. Within living memory we responded to a sneak attack by interning American citizens because they, or their parents, or their grandparents were from Japan. In retrospect, those actions were not only unjust and morally wrong, they were unnecessary and did nothing to protect us.

The horrific events of 9/11 tempted me to think that interning people without due process might be the thing to do. Maybe we do need to sacrifice personal liberties to be safe, but then I remember that generations of Americans bled and died to create and protect the rule of law, and I wonder: If we ignore it now, how will we ever get it back?

Like Tinkerbell, the rule of law has been seriously injured by doubt. Those who believe in it must stand up and say—I must say—I believe in the rule of law and will not accept its being taken away. I believe that we are not so weak, so impotent, or so frightened that we must give it up or perish. I believe that those few who have harmed us, and who will do so again, are not so powerful that we must abandon the very thing that makes it worth being an American.

MICHAEL MULLANE *is a law professor and director of the Law School Legal Clinic at the University of Arkansas in Fayetteville. He has also worked in private practice in Arizona and in a legal clinic in Maine. Born into a military family, Mullane was a Navy aviator during the Vietnam War.*

Getting Angry Can Be a Good Thing

Cecilia Muñoz

I BELIEVE THAT A LITTLE OUTRAGE CAN take you a long way.

I remember the exact moment when I discovered outrage as a kind of fuel. It was about 1980. I was seventeen, the daughter of Bolivian immigrants growing up in suburban Detroit. After a dinner table conversation with my family about the wars going on in Central America and the involvement of the United States (my country by birth and my parents' country by choice), a good friend said the thing that set me off. He told me that he thought the U.S. might someday go to war somewhere in Latin America. He looked me in the eye and told me that if it happens, he believes my parents belong in an internment camp just like the Japanese-Americans during World War II.

Now this was someone who knew us, who had sat at our table and knew how American we are. We are a little exotic maybe, but it never occurred to me that we were anything but an American family. For my friend, as for many others, there will always be doubt as to whether we really belong in this country, which is our home, enough doubt to justify taking away our freedom. My outrage that day became the propellant of my life, driving me straight to the civil rights movement, where I've worked ever since.

I guess outrage got me pretty far. I found jobs in the immigrant rights movement. I moved to Washington to work as an advocate. I found plenty more to be angry about along the way and built something of a reputation for being strident. Someone once sent my mom an article about my work. She was proud and everything, but wanted to know why her baby was described as "ferocious."

Anger has a way, though, of hollowing out your insides. In my first job, if we helped fifty immigrant families in a day, the faces of the five who didn't qualify haunted my dreams at night. When I helped pass a bill in Congress to help Americans reunite with their immigrant families, I could only think of my cousin who didn't qualify and who had to wait another decade to get her immigration papers.

It's like that every day. You have victories, but your defeats outnumber them by far, and you remember the names and faces of those who lost. I still have the article about the farmworker who took his life after we lost a political fight. I have not forgotten his name—and not just because his last name was the same as mine. His story reminds me of why I do this work and how little I can really do.

I am deeply familiar with that hollow place that outrage carves in your soul. I've fed off of it to sustain my work for many years. But it hasn't eaten me away completely, maybe because the hollow place gets filled with other, more powerful things like compassion, faith, family, music, the goodness of people around me. These things fill me up and temper my outrage with a deep sense of gratitude that I have the privilege of doing my small part to make things better.

Cecilia Muñoz *is vice president of the Office of Research, Advocacy, and Legislation at the National Council of La Raza. Born in Detroit to Bolivian immigrants, she has worked on behalf of Hispanic-Americans. Muñoz was named a MacArthur Fellow in 2000.*

Mysterious Connections That Link Us Together

Azar Nafisi

I BELIEVE IN EMPATHY. I believe in the kind of empathy that is created through imagination and through intimate, personal relationships.

I am a writer and a teacher so much of my time is spent interpreting stories and connecting to other individuals. It is the urge to know more about ourselves and others that creates empathy. Through imagination and our desire for rapport, we transcend our limitations, freshen our eyes, and are able to look at ourselves and the world through a new and alternative lens.

Whenever I think of the word "empathy," I think of a small boy named Huckleberry Finn contemplating his friend and runaway slave, Jim. Huck asks himself whether he should give Jim up or not. Huck was told in Sunday school that people who let slaves go free go to "everlasting fire." But then, Huck says he imagines he and Jim in "the day and nighttime, sometimes moonlight, sometimes storms, and we a-floating along, talking and singing and laughing." Huck remembers Jim and their friendship and warmth. He imagines Jim not as a slave but as a human being and he decides that, "alright, then, I'll go to hell."

What Huck rejects is not religion but an attitude of self-righteousness and inflexibility. I remember this particular scene out of *Huck Finn* so vividly today because I associate it with a difficult time in my own life. In the early 1980s, when I taught at the University of Tehran, I, like many others, was expelled. I was very surprised to discover that my staunchest allies were two students who were very active at the university's powerful Muslim Students' Association. These young men and I had engaged in very passionate and heated arguments. I had fiercely opposed their ideological stances. But that didn't stop them from defending me. When I ran into one of them after my expulsion, I thanked him for his support. "We are not as rigid as you imagine us to be, Professor Nafisi," he responded. "Remember your own lectures on Huck Finn? Let's just say, he is not the only one who can risk going to hell!"

This experience in my life reinforces my belief in the mysterious connections that link individuals to each other despite their vast differences. No amount of political correctness can make us empathize with a child left orphaned in Darfur or a woman taken to a football stadium in Kabul and shot to death because she is improperly dressed. Only curiosity about the fate of others, the ability to put ourselves in their shoes, and the will to enter their world through the magic of imagination creates this shock of recognition. Without this empathy there can be no genuine dialogue, and we as individuals and nations will remain isolated and alien, segregated and fragmented.

I believe that it is only through empathy that the pain experienced by an Algerian woman, a North Korean dissident, a Rwandan child, or an Iraqi prisoner becomes real to me and not just passing news. And it is at times like this when I ask myself, am I prepared—like Huck Finn—to give up Sunday school heaven for the kind of hell that Huck chose?

Iranian-born writer Azar Nafisi *was fired from the University of Tehran for refusing to wear a veil. Her book,* Reading Lolita in Tehran, *is based on the years she secretly taught literature to female students in her home. Nafisi now works at the Johns Hopkins School of Advanced International Studies.*

The Making of Poems

Gregory Orr

I BELIEVE IN POETRY AS A WAY of surviving the emotional chaos, spiritual confusions, and traumatic events that come with being alive.

When I was twelve years old, I was responsible for the death of my younger brother in a hunting accident. I held the rifle that killed him. In a single moment, my world changed forever. I felt grief, terror, shame, and despair more deeply than I could ever have imagined. In the aftermath, no one in my shattered family could speak to me about my brother's death, and their silence left me alone with all my agonizing emotions. And under those emotions, something even more terrible: a knowledge that all the easy meanings I had lived by until then had been suddenly and utterly abolished.

One consequence of traumatic violence is that it isolates its victims. It can cut us off from other people, cutting us off from our own emotional lives until we go numb and move through the world as if only half alive. As a young person, I found something to set against my growing sense of isolation and numbness: the making of poems.

When I write a poem, I process experience. I take what's inside me—the raw, chaotic material of feeling or memory—and translate it into words and then shape those words into the rhythmical language we call a poem. This process brings me a kind of wild joy. Before, I was powerless and passive in the face of my confusion, but now I am active: the powerful shaper of my experience. I am transforming it into a lucid meaning.

Because poems are meanings, and even the saddest poem I write is proof that I want to survive. And therefore it represents an affirmation of life in all its complexities and contradictions.

An additional miracle comes to me as the maker of poems: Because poems can be shared between poet and audience, they also become a further triumph over human isolation.

Whenever I read a poem that moves me, I know I'm not alone in the world. I feel a connection to the person who wrote it, knowing that he or she has gone through something similar to what I've experienced, or felt something like what I have felt. And their poem gives me hope and courage, because I know that they survived, that their life force was strong enough to turn experience into words and shape it into meaning and then bring it toward me to share. The gift of their poem enters deeply into me and helps me live and believe in living.

GREGORY ORR *teaches at the University of Virginia. He is the author of a memoir,* The Blessing; *a collection of essays,* Poetry As Survival; *as well as nine books of poetry, including* Concerning The Book That Is The Body Of The Beloved. *Orr lives in Charlottesville, Virginia, with his wife, the painter Trisha Orr.*

We Are Each Other's Business

Eboo Patel

I AM AN AMERICAN MUSLIM. I believe in pluralism. In the Holy Quran, God tells us, "I created you into diverse nations and tribes that you may come to know one another." I believe America is humanity's best opportunity to make God's wish that we come to know one another a reality.

In my office hangs Norman Rockwell's illustration *Freedom of Worship*. A Muslim holding a Quran in his hands stands near a Catholic woman fingering her rosary. Other figures have their hands folded in prayer and their eyes filled with piety. They stand shoulder-to-shoulder facing the same direction, comfortable with the presence of one another and yet apart. It is a vivid depiction of a group living in peace with its diversity, yet not exploring it.

We live in a world where the forces that seek to divide us are strong. To overcome them, we must do more than simply stand next to one another in silence.

I attended high school in the western suburbs of Chicago. The group I ate lunch with included a Jew, a Mormon, a Hindu, a Catholic, and a Lutheran. We were all devout to a degree, but we almost never talked about religion. Somebody would announce at the table that they couldn't eat a certain kind of food, or any food at all, for a period of time. We all knew religion hovered behind this, but nobody ever offered any explanation deeper than "my mom said," and nobody ever asked for one.

A few years after we graduated, my Jewish friend from the lunchroom reminded me of an experience we both wish had never happened. A group of thugs in our high school had taken to scrawling anti-Semitic slurs on classroom desks and shouting them in the hallway.

I did not confront them. I did not comfort my Jewish friend. Instead I averted my eyes from their bigotry, and I avoided the eyes of my friend because I couldn't stand to face him.

My friend told me he feared coming to school those days, and he felt abandoned as he watched his close friends do nothing. Hearing him tell me of his suffering—and my complicity—is the single most humiliating experience of my life.

My friend needed more than my silent presence at the lunch table. I realize now that to believe in pluralism means I need the courage to act on it. Action is what separates a belief from an opinion. Beliefs are imprinted through actions.

In the words of the American poet Gwendolyn Brooks: "We are each other's business; we are each other's harvest; we are each other's magnitude and bond."

I cannot go back in time and take away the suffering of my Jewish friend, but through action I can prevent it from happening to others.

Eboo Patel is the founder and executive director of the Interfaith Youth Core, a Chicago-based organization fostering the international interfaith youth movement. He lectures worldwide on youth and religion and was a keynote speaker at the 2004 Nobel Peace Prize Forum. In 2002, Utne magazine named Patel one of their "30 under 30 Young Visionaries."

The 50-Percent Theory of Life

Steve Porter

I BELIEVE IN THE 50-PERCENT THEORY. Half the time things are better than normal; the other half, they are worse. I believe life is a pendulum swing. It takes time and experience to understand what normal is, and that gives me the perspective to deal with the surprises of the future.

Let's benchmark the parameters: Yes, I will die. I've dealt with the deaths of both parents, a best friend, a beloved boss, and cherished pets. Some of these deaths have been violent, before my eyes, or slow and agonizing. Bad stuff, and it belongs at the bottom of the scale.

Then there are those high points: romance and marriage

to the right person; having a child and doing those Dad things, like coaching my son's baseball team, paddling around the creek in the boat while he's swimming with the dogs, discovering his compassion so deep it manifests even in his kindness to snails, his imagination so vivid he builds a spaceship from a scattered pile of LEGOs.

But there is a vast meadow of life in the middle, where the bad and the good flip-flop acrobatically. This is what convinces me to believe in the 50-percent theory.

One spring I planted corn too early in a bottomland so flood-prone that neighbors laughed. I felt chagrined at the wasted effort. Summer turned brutal—the worst heat wave and drought in my lifetime. The air conditioner died, the well went dry, the marriage ended, the job lost, the money gone. I was living lyrics from a country tune—music I loathed. Only a surging Kansas City Royals team, bound for their first World Series, buoyed my spirits.

Looking back on that horrible summer, I soon understood that all succeeding good things merely offset the bad. Worse than normal wouldn't last long. I am owed and savor the halcyon times. They reinvigorate me for the next nasty surprise and offer assurance that I can thrive. The 50-percent theory even helps me see hope beyond my Royals' recent slump, a field of struggling rookies sown so that some year soon we can reap an October harvest.

Oh, yeah, the corn crop? For that one blistering summer, the ground moisture was just right, planting early allowed pollination before heat withered the tops, and the lack of rain spared the standing corn from floods. That winter my crib overflowed with corn—fat, healthy three-to-a-stalk ears filled with kernels from heel to tip—while my neighbors' fields yielded only brown, empty husks.

Although plantings past may have fallen below the 50-percent expectation, and they probably will again in the future, I am still sustained by the crop that flourishes during the drought.

STEVE PORTER *lives on western Missouri farmland that has been in his family since the 1840s. He has planted one corn crop so far. In addition to coaching and watching baseball, he works in community relations for the Missouri Department of Transportation.*

The America I Believe In

Colin Powell

I BELIEVE IN AMERICA, AND I BELIEVE in our people.

Later this month, I will be participating in a ceremony at Ellis Island, where I will receive copies of the ship manifest and the immigration documents that record the arrival in America of my mother, Maud Ariel McKoy, from Jamaica aboard the motor ship *Turialba* in 1923. My father, Luther Powell, had arrived three years earlier at the Port of Philadelphia.

They met in New York City, married, became Americans, and raised a family. By their hard work and their love for this country, they enriched this nation and helped it grow and thrive. They instilled in their children and grandchildren that same love of country and a spirit of optimism.

My family's story is a common one, one that has been told by millions of Americans. We are a land of immigrants: a nation that has been touched by every nation and we, in turn, touch every nation. And we are touched not just by immigrants but by the visitors who come to America and return home to tell of their experiences.

I believe that our greatest strength in dealing with the world is the openness of our society and the welcoming nature of our people. A good stay in our country is the best public diplomacy tool we have.

After 9/11 we realized that our country's openness was also its vulnerability. We needed to protect ourselves by knowing who was coming into the country, for what purpose, and to know when they left. This was entirely appropriate and reasonable.

Unfortunately, to many foreigners we gave the impression that we were no longer a welcoming nation. They started to go to schools and hospitals in other countries, and frankly, they started to take their business elsewhere. We can't allow that to happen. Our attitude has to be: We are glad you are here. We must be careful, but we must not be afraid.

As I traveled the world as secretary of state, I encountered anti-American sentiment. But I also encountered an underlying respect and affection for America. People still want to come here. Refugees who have no home at all know that America is their land of dreams. Even with added scrutiny, people line up at our embassies to apply to come here.

You see, I believe that the America of 2005 is the same America that brought Maud Ariel McKoy and Luther Powell to these shores, and so many millions of others. An America that each day gives new immigrants the same gift that my parents received. An America that lives by a Constitution that inspires freedom and democracy around the world. An America with a big, open, charitable heart that reaches out to people in need around the world. An America that sometimes seems confused and is always noisy—that noise has a name; it's called democracy, and we use it to work through our confusion. An America that is still the beacon of light to the darkest corner of the world.

Last year I met with a group of Brazilian exchange students who had spent a few weeks in America. I asked them to tell me about their experience here. One young girl told me about the night the twelve students went to a fast-food restaurant in Chicago. They ate and then realized they did not have enough money to pay the bill. They were way short. Frightened, they finally told the waitress of their problem. She went away and she came back in a little while, saying, "I talked to the manager and he said, 'It's okay.'" The students were still concerned because they thought the waitress might have to pay for it out of her salary. She smiled and she said, "No, the manager said he is glad you are here in the United States. He hopes you are having a good time; he hopes you are learning all about us. He said that it's on him."

It is a story that those young Brazilian kids have told over and over about America. That's the America I believe in; that's the America the world wants to believe in.

COLIN POWELL *spent thirty-five years in the military, rising from ROTC in college to become a four-star general and chairman of the Joint Chiefs of Staff during the 1991 Gulf War. He has worked in the administrations of six presidents, including serving as secretary of state from 2001 to 2005.*

The Real Consequences of Justice

Frederic Reamer

Last Tuesday morning I stared across the table at a woman with severe scars lining her otherwise gentle face. Her raging husband carved those scars and sliced off her ear when she told him she wanted a divorce.

I'm a member of the Rhode Island Parole Board. Month after month—thirteen years' worth of months—I've met with criminals and victims. Immediately before my colleagues and I conduct parole hearings for the criminals, we meet with their victims if they wish to tell us their stories.

Every time I walk into those hearing rooms I retest my belief in justice. I do my best to balance my concern for public safety and my faith that some offenders truly have the ability to redeem themselves. And I can't ignore my wish to punish those criminals who willfully ruined another person's life.

On hearing days, nearly always, the victims plead with us to keep the prisoner behind bars. All morning long I hear their gut-wrenching stories of murder, rape, child molestation, armed robbery, and domestic violence.

The victims return to their lives—which are often in shambles—and hours later I find myself face-to-face with the perpetrators. I settle in to hear what the prisoners have to say. Often their stories are filled with regret, with hope, and lots of promises.

These back-to-back encounters force me to confront what I really believe about people's fundamental rights. I'm proud to be part of a system like ours—as imperfect as it is. The system does most of its work in the open and takes seriously the rights of both victims and the accused.

But the truth is, I struggle to balance these clanging, colliding rights. Only an hour after meeting with the woman with jagged scars on her face, I met with her offender. In his khaki inmate uniform, this monster explained with impressive insight and remorse how he had mishandled his failing marriage. The inmate showed me, with heartfelt words, the fruits of his hard emotional labor while in prison—what he had learned in treatment programs and from his own soul-searching. All of a sudden, he didn't seem quite so monstrous.

So, how do I administer justice? I believe that justice can't be shaped by simplistic formulas. Rather, justice happens when real human beings sort through a jumble of laws, rules, conflicting stories, and plain old instinct.

Sitting there in front of me that morning was what justice is all about. The victim heaved and sobbed, fearing the prisoner's release. But both of us knew that the inmate would walk out of that prison someday—after all, the judge did not impose a life sentence. The question I had to answer was whether he would walk out the front gate on my watch.

Administering justice is not theoretical. There are real consequences every time I answer the question: What do I believe?

FREDERIC REAMER *is a professor at the School of Social Work at Rhode Island College. His research and teaching explore mental health, criminal justice, and professional ethics. Reamer has served on the Rhode Island Parole Board since 1992.*

There Is More to Life than My Life

Jamaica Ritcher

My daughter Maia is two, and has just asked about our cat. Our cat is dead. Maia knows this—what she's wondering is where he's gone and what has happened to him, now that he no longer meows beneath her kitchen chair, impatient for the drips off her spoon.

This is the moment I realize: I need to know what I believe.

My parents were straightforward in admitting they didn't know what happens when we die. As a child, I probably lost a solid year of sleep pondering that enormous mystery: Bone-still under the covers I lay awake picturing my future of eternal nothingness and wracked by the tragedy of no more Me. The subject still haunts me. I'd like Maia's attitude to be slightly healthier. This is what I bring to composing an answer to her question about the cat.

After a weighty pause I tell my daughter that Martin (the cat) is out in the field. I tell her that when animals, including people, die, they are usually put into the ground and that their bodies become the grasses, flowers, and trees. I pass my hand over Maia's blonde curls, gently touch a rosy cheek, and check her reaction. She appears untroubled. She seems thrilled by the thought of one day becoming a flower.

I am stunned. In this exchange, I actually realize what I believe, as if so many fragments from my life—camping trips and nature walks, pangs of sympathy, awe toward the crashing sea and towering skyscraper, love, science class, motherhood—have suddenly converged into one, unified conviction: not that I'm destined for plant fertilizer, but that there is more to life than my life. I am not the lonely human, plunked down on earth to aimlessly wander. I am a part of that earth and not going anywhere—just like the spider up in the corner, the dust on the sill, and the cat I buried in the backyard. I watch Maia mull things over while she munches her Cheerios. I feel an unfamiliar calm. I feel connected. I am humbled and, what's more, happy. Life, death, both are all around me, within my every breath.

Later, I reach for my daughter's hand and we muddy our shoes with a springtime walk. Together, we see new leaves glowing against the sun, green hillsides shimmering with the breeze, the bright purple bursts of lupine. And it's okay if there is nothing beyond this, because there is this: life, everlasting, in the bloom of every flower.

> *A native of northern California, JAMAICA RITCHER has enjoyed the outdoors since she was a child. In addition to being an avid camper, she studied cultural anthropology and natural science in college. Ritcher and her family now live in Australia, where her husband is doing postdoctoral research in plant biology.*

Tomorrow Will Be a Better Day

Josh Rittenberg

I'm sixteen. The other night, while I was busy thinking about important social issues, like what to do over the weekend and who to do it with, I overheard my parents talking about my future. My dad was upset—not the usual stuff that he and Mom and, I guess, a lot of parents worry about, like which college I'm going to, how far away it is from home, and how much it's going to cost. Instead, he was upset about the world his generation is turning over to mine, a world he fears has a dark and difficult future—if it has a future at all.

He sounded like this: "There will be a pandemic that kills millions, a devastating energy crisis, a horrible worldwide depression, and a nuclear explosion set off in anger."

As I lay on the living room couch, eavesdropping on their conversation, starting to worry about the future my father was describing, I found myself looking at some old family photos. There was a picture of my grandfather in his Citadel uniform. He was a member of the class of 1942, the war class. Next to his picture were photos of my great-grandparents, Ellis Island immigrants. Seeing those pictures made me feel a lot better. I believe tomorrow will be better than today—that the world my generation grows into is going to get better, not worse. Those pictures helped me understand why.

I considered some of the awful things my grandparents and great-grandparents had seen in their lifetimes: two world wars, killer flu, segregation, a nuclear bomb. But they saw other things, too, better things: the end of two world wars, the polio vaccine, passage of the civil rights laws. They even saw the Red Sox win the World Series—twice.

I believe that my generation will see better things, too—that we will witness the time when AIDS is cured and cancer is defeated; when the Middle East will find peace and Africa grain, and the Cubs win the World Series—probably, only once. I will see things as inconceivable to me today as a moon shot was to my grandfather when he was sixteen, or the Internet to my father when he was sixteen.

Ever since I was a little kid, whenever I've had a lousy day, my dad would put his arm around me and promise me that "tomorrow will be a better day." I challenged my father once: "How do you know that?" He said, "I just do." I believed him. My great-grandparents believed that, and my grandparents, and so do I.

As I listened to my dad talking that night, so worried about what the future holds for me and my generation, I wanted to put my arm around him and tell him what he always told me, "Don't worry, Dad. Tomorrow will be a better day." This, I believe.

Josh Rittenberg *attends Columbia Grammar and Preparatory School in Manhattan, where he plays baseball and guitar and sings tenor in an a cappella group. Inspired by the TV show* Law and Order, *Rittenberg cofounded his school's Mock Trial Club.* Newsday *published an essay he wrote about excessive homework.*

Free Minds and Hearts at Work

Jackie Robinson,
as featured in the 1950s series

At the beginning of the World Series of 1947, I experienced a completely new emotion, when the national anthem was played. This time, I thought, it is being played for me, as much as for anyone else. This is organized major-league baseball, and I am standing here with all the others; and everything that takes place includes me.

About a year later, I went to Atlanta, Georgia, to play in an exhibition game. On the field, for the first time in Atlanta, there were Negroes and whites. Other Negroes, besides me. And I thought: What I have always believed has come to be.

And what is it that I have always believed? First, that

imperfections are human. But that wherever human beings were given room to breathe and time to think, those imperfections would disappear, no matter how slowly. I do *not* believe that we have found or even approached perfection. That is not necessarily in the scheme of human events. Handicaps, stumbling blocks, prejudices—all of these are imperfect. Yet, they have to be reckoned with because *they* are in the scheme of human events.

Whatever obstacles I found made me fight all the harder. But it would have been impossible for me to fight at all, except that I was sustained by the personal and deep-rooted belief that my fight had a chance. It had a chance because it took place in a free society. Not once was I forced to face and fight an immovable object. Not once was the situation so cast-iron rigid that I had no chance at all. Free minds and human hearts were at work all around me; and so there was the probability of improvement.

I look at my children now and know that I must still prepare them to meet obstacles and prejudices. But I can tell them, too, that they will never face *some* of these prejudices because other people have gone before them. And to myself I can say that, because progress is unalterable, many of today's dogmas will have vanished by the time they grow into adults. I can say to my children: There is a chance for you. No guarantee, but a chance.

And this chance has come to be, because there is nothing static with free people. There is no Middle Ages logic so strong that it can stop the human tide from flowing forward. I do *not* believe that every person, in every walk of life, can succeed in spite of any handicap. That would be perfection. But I do believe—and with every fiber in me—that what I was able to attain came to be because we put behind us (no matter how slowly) the dogmas of the past to discover the truth of today, and perhaps find the greatness of tomorrow.

I believe in the human race. I believe in the warm heart. I believe in man's integrity. I believe in the goodness of a free society. And I believe that the society can remain good only as long as we are willing to fight for it—and to fight against whatever imperfections may exist.

My fight was against the barriers that kept Negroes out of baseball. This was the area where I found imperfection, and where I was best able to fight. And I fought because I knew it was not doomed to be a losing fight. It couldn't be a losing fight—not when it took place in a free society.

And, in the largest sense, I believe that what I did was done for me—and that my faith in God sustained me in my fight. And that what was done for me must and will be done for others.

In 1947, JACKIE ROBINSON pioneered the integration of American professional athletics by becoming the first black player in major-league baseball. During his ten seasons with the Brooklyn Dodgers, he played on six World Series teams and was voted the National League's Most Valuable Player in 1949.

Growth That Starts from Thinking

Eleanor Roosevelt,
as featured in the 1950s series

It seems to me a very difficult thing to put into words the beliefs we hold and what they make you do in your life. I think I was fortunate because I grew up in a family where there was a very deep religious feeling. I don't think it was spoken of a great deal. It was more or less taken for granted that everybody held certain beliefs and needed certain reinforcement of their own strength and that that came through your belief in God and your knowledge of prayer.

But as I grew older I questioned a great many of the things that I knew very well my grandmother who brought me up had taken for granted. And I think I might have been quite a difficult person to live with if it hadn't been for the fact that my husband once said it didn't do you any harm to learn those things, so why not let your children learn them? When they grow up, they'll think things out for themselves.

And that gave me a feeling that perhaps that's what we all had to do—think out for ourselves what we could believe and how we could live by it. And so I came to the conclusion that you had to use this life to develop the very best that you could develop.

I don't know whether I believe in a future life. I believe that all that you go through here must have some value; therefore, there must be some *reason*. And there must be some "going on." How exactly that happens, I've never been able to decide. There is a future—that I'm sure of. But *how*, that I don't know. And I came to feel that it didn't really matter very much because whatever the future held, you'd have to face it when you came to it, just as whatever life holds, you have to face it in exactly the same way. And the important thing was that you never let down doing the best that you were able to do—it might be poor because you might not have very much within you to give, or to help other people with, or to live your life with. But as long as you did the very best that you were able to do, then that was what you were put here to do, and that was what you were accomplishing by being here.

And so I have tried to follow that out—and not to worry about the future or what was going to happen. I think I am pretty much of a fatalist. You have to accept whatever comes and the only important thing is that you meet it with courage and with the best that you have to give.

> ELEANOR ROOSEVELT, *wife of Franklin D. Roosevelt, was active in Democratic politics and helped shape her husband's New Deal programs while he was president. Considered one of the most active and influential First Ladies in U.S. history, she advocated racial equality, women's rights, and world peace.*

The Artistry in Hidden Talents

Mel Rusnov

I BELIEVE IN CULTIVATING HIDDEN TALENTS, buried and unrelated to what we do for a living.

In ordinary life, I'm a civil engineer. I make a satisfying, comfortable living working quietly in my cubicle. But in my other life, I am a pianist, bringing to life, with my own hands, the genius of Bach, Mozart, and Chopin.

While earning my engineering degree, I worked as a waitress in the dining hall of a retirement community. One day during a break, I discovered a piano in a meeting room. I sat down to play a few Bach Two-Part Inventions. Those crisp, driving rhythms and harmonics flew out into the hallways. Residents, numb from ceaseless easy-listening radio, tentatively peeked in, then sat to listen.

Disbelieving, they saw plain, old, invisible Mel, the lunch waitress. "She plays the piano!" "Where did you study?" "How long have you played?" "Can you play Rachmaninoff?"

They no longer wanted me to quickly and quietly disappear from their dining tables. "Mel, wait a minute. Who do you think was better, Gould or Horowitz?" I answered "Gould," and a raging debate ensued.

For over twenty years, absorbed in my engineering career, I let my musical life die, but I was always reminded of it when I'd encounter the secret creative life of others. At a holiday concert, I heard a tenor voice so glorious, it brought tears to my eyes. It was the sweetest, most touching performance of "Silent Night" I had ever heard. This masterful voice belonged to a colleague, Steve, with whom I had worked for years, side-by-side in adjoining cubicles.

I had narrowly defined him, and so many others, by their occupations. Since I had let myself get consumed by my job, too tired and spent for anything else, I assumed all other hardworking people had, too. But Steve's artistry reminded me of my own hidden talent. I began to practice again and started taking lessons from an inspiring teacher who pressures me every week to keep at it, play better, get to that next higher level.

One time, feeling bold, I played a Mozart Sonata in an airport lobby, between connecting flights. People slowed down or even stopped to listen; readers looked up from their chairs. I saw smiles and heard a smattering of applause. I thought: No one smiled and clapped after my presentation on the site engineering for a new strip mall.

I believe we are more than the inhabitants of our cubicles, more than engineers or even parents, husbands, and wives. I believe we are transformed and connected by the power and beauty of our creativity.

MEL RUSNOV *is a civil engineer in Woodbury, Connecticut. Her love of music came from her father, who played in a Croatian folk group and who took her to orchestra concerts in their hometown of Cleveland. In addition to playing the piano, Rusnov enjoys tutoring local high school students in math.*

My Fellow Worms

Carl Sandburg,
as featured in the 1950s series

The man who sits down and searches himself for his answer to the question "What Do I Believe?" is either going to write a book or a few well-chosen thoughts on what he thinks it might be healthy for mankind to be thinking about in the present tribulations and turmoils. I believe in getting up in the morning with a serene mind and a heart holding many hopes. And so large a number of my fellow worms in the dust believe the same that there is no use putting stress on it.

I can remember many years ago, a beautiful woman in Santa Fe saying, "I don't see how anybody can study astronomy and have ambition enough to get up in the morning." She was putting a comic twist on what an insignificant speck of animate stardust each of us is amid cotillions of billion-year constellations.

I believe in humility, though my confession and exposition of the humility I believe in would run into an old fashioned two- or three-hour sermon. Also I believe in pride, knowing well that the deadliest of the seven deadly sins is named as pride. I believe in a pride that prays ever for an awareness of that borderline where, unless watchful of yourself, you cross over into arrogance, into vanity, into mirror gazing, into misuse and violation of the sacred portions of your personality.

No single brief utterance of Lincoln is more portentous than the line he wrote to a federal authority in Louisiana. "I shall do nothing in malice, for what I deal with is too vast for malicious dealing."

Now I believe in platitudes, when they serve, especially that battered and hard-worn antique, "Eternal vigilance is the pride of liberty." Hand in hand with freedom goes responsibility. I believe that free men over the world cherish the earth as cradle and tomb, the handiwork of their Maker, the possession of the family of man.

I believe freedom comes the hard way—by ceaseless groping, toil, struggle—even by fiery trial and agony.

> *Known as a "people's poet,"* Carl Sandburg *was a voice of the workingman of industrial America. He also worked as a biographer, lecturer, newspaper columnist, and folksinger. Sandburg won a Pulitzer Prize in 1940 for part of his biography of Abraham Lincoln, and again in 1951 for his poetry.*

When Children Are Wanted

Margaret Sanger,
as featured in the 1950s series

This I Believe, first of all: that all our basic convictions must be tested and transmuted in the crucible of experience—and sometimes the more bitter the experience, the more valid the purified belief.

As a child, one of a large family, I learned that the thing I did best was the thing I liked to do. This realization of doing and getting results was what I have later called an awakening consciousness.

There is an old Indian proverb which has inspired me in the work of my adult life. "Build thou beyond thyself, but first be sure that thou thyself be strong and healthy in body and mind." Yes, to build, to work, to plan to do something, not for yourself, not for your own benefit, but "beyond thyself"—and when this idea permeates the mind you begin to think in terms of a future.

I began to think of a world beyond myself when I first took an interest in nursing the sick. As a nurse, I was in contact with the ill and the infirm. I knew something about the health and disease of bodies, but for a long time I was baffled at the tremendous personal problems of life, of marriage, of living, and just of being. Here indeed was a challenge to "build beyond thyself." But where was I to begin? I found the answer at every door. I began to believe there was something I could do toward increasing an understanding of these basic human problems. To build beyond myself, I must first tap all inner resources of stamina, of courage, of resolution within myself. I was prepared to face opposition, even ridicule, denunciation. But I also had to prepare myself, in defense of these unpopular beliefs; I had to prepare myself to face courts and even prisons. But I resolved to stand up, alone if necessary, against all the entrenched forces which opposed me.

I started my battle some forty years ago. The women and mothers whom I wanted to help also wanted to help me. They, too, wanted to build beyond the self, in creating healthy children and bringing them up in life to be happy and useful citizens. I believed it was my duty to place motherhood on a higher level than enslavement and accident. I was convinced we must care about people; we must reach out to help them in their despair.

For these beliefs I was denounced, arrested. I was in and out of police courts and higher courts, and indictments hung over my life for several years. But nothing could alter my beliefs. Because I saw these as truths, and I stubbornly stuck to my convictions.

No matter what it may cost in health, in misunderstanding, in sacrifice, something had to be done, and I felt that I was called by the force of circumstances to do it. Because of my philosophy and my work, my life has been enriched and full. My interests have expanded from local conditions and needs to a world horizon, where peace on earth may be achieved when children are wanted before they are conceived. A new consciousness will take place, a new race will be born to bring peace on earth. This belief has withstood the crucible of my life's joyous struggle. It remains my basic belief today.

This I believe—at the end, as at the beginning, of my long crusade for the future of the human race.

> MARGARET SANGER *founded the first birth control clinic in the United States in 1916, at a time when it was illegal to publish and distribute information on contraception. A lifelong advocate for birth control and women's rights, she founded the American Birth Control League in 1921, which later became the Planned Parenthood Federation of America.*

Jazz Is the Sound of God Laughing

~

Colleen Shaddox

Jazz is the sound of God laughing. And I believe in it.

I came to know jazz as a child, stretched out beneath my uncle's baby grand. I would lie there for hours drawing while Uncle Charlie practiced. I could feel the vibrations go right through me, filling me up with jazz. I felt happier in that room than anywhere on the planet. A lot of that had to do with being admitted to the inner sanctum of my favorite grown-up. But in retrospect, I realize it was also about the music.

I believe in the fundamental optimism of jazz. Consider the first four notes of "Rhapsody in Blue." Can you hear it? It's saying, "Something monumental is going to happen. Something that's never happened before. And you are alive to witness it."

Jazz is always like that. Even the songs that take you to despair lift you. That's because the music remembers where it came from, from people kidnapped and enslaved. It came from a humanity that was attacked a thousand different ways every day, but never defeated. It's the People's Music.

I remember my uncle's hands on the piano. His fingers always had tiny burns on them, a hazard of his job as a welder. He spent his days at the Brooklyn Navy Yard building the ships that won the second World War. He spent his nights playing piano and sax for couples who glided and gyrated across the city's polished floors.

In jazz, anybody can sit in. It's dogma-free, which allows the music to take more than its share of detours. This forces you to have faith. Faith that if you keep moving forward, you'll get there.

As an adult, cancer tested my faith. I was not afraid of dying—after all, that's only a key change—but I was terrified of leaving my baby without a mother. Walking in the woods with my son, who by no coincidence bears my uncle's name, I was fighting back tears. Charlie noticed some honeybees and started imitating their sound. All of a sudden, he sang "Buzz. Buzz, buzz, buzz-buzz." Those are the opening notes of "Green Dolphin Street," a jazz standard that I'd wager few three-year-olds know.

Thankfully, I lived. But if I hadn't, I learned that day that I could never leave my Charlie, any more than Uncle Charlie had ever left me. The three of us shared a treasure passed through generations. My baby knew jazz, which is the same as knowing that the universe carries us all toward joyful reunions.

There are some ugly noises in the universe today. At any given moment I can turn on my television and watch people trampling over each other to gain the moral high ground. Sometimes, I despair. But on good days, I turn off the television and put on some Oscar Peterson. And I whisper a prayer for America to remember that we are "Green Onions," "String of Pearls," "A Sunday Kind of Love," and "The Dirty Boogie." We are the people of Louis, George, Miles, and Wynton. We are the jazz people.

We'll get there. I believe it.

COLLEEN SHADDOX *says she is living proof that you can be tone deaf and still love music. She is a writer, editor, and owner of a public relations firm that serves health care companies and nonprofit organizations. Shaddox lives in her native Connecticut with her husband, son, and dog.*

There Is No Such Thing as Too Much Barbecue

Jason Sheehan

AFTER LISTENING TO THE RESULTS OF THIS PROJECT for several weeks, I knew I could do three minutes, too. Certainly not on world peace or the search for meaning in an increasingly distracted world or anything as grave and serious as all that, but on a belief just as true.

I believe in barbecue. As soul food and comfort food and health food, as a cuisine of both solace and celebration. When I'm feeling good, I want barbecue. And when I'm feeling bad, I just want barbecue more. I believe in barbecue in all its regional derivations, in its ethnic translations, in forms that range from white-tablecloth presentations of cunningly sauced costillas, to Chinese take-out spareribs that stain your fingers red, to the most authentic product of the tar-paper rib shacks of the Deep South. I believe that like sunshine and great sex, no day is bad that has barbecue in it.

I believe in the art of generations of pit-men working in relative obscurity to keep alive the craft of slow-smoking as it's been practiced for as long as there's been fire. A barbecue cook must have an intimate understanding of his work, the physics of fire and convection, the hard science of meat and heat and smoke—and then forget it all to achieve a sort of gut-level, Zen instinct for the process.

I believe that barbecue drives culture, not the other way around. Some of the first blows struck for equality and civil rights in the Deep South were made not in the courtrooms or schools or on buses, but in the barbecue shacks. There were dining rooms, backyards, and roadhouse juke joints in the South that were integrated long before any other public places.

I believe that good barbecue requires no décor, and that the best barbecue exists despite its trappings. Paper plates are okay in a barbecue joint. And paper napkins. And plastic silverware. And I believe that any place with a menu longer than can fit on a single page—or better yet, just a chalkboard—is coming dangerously close to putting on airs.

I believe that good barbecue needs sides the way good blues need rhythm, and that there is only one rule: Serve whatever you like, but whatever you serve, make it fresh. Have someone's mama in the back doing the "taters" and hush puppies and sweet tea, because Mama will know what she's doing—or at least know better than some assembly-line worker bagging up powdered mashed potatoes by the ton.

I believe that proper barbecue ought to come in significant portions. Skinny people can eat barbecue, and do, but the kitchen should cook for a fat man who hasn't eaten since breakfast. My leftovers should last for days.

I believe that if you don't get sauce under your nails when you're eating, you're doing it wrong. I believe that if you don't ruin your shirt, you're not trying hard enough.

I believe—*I know*—there is no such thing as too much barbecue. Good, bad, or in-between, old-fashioned pit-smoked or high-tech and modern; it doesn't matter. Existing without gimmickry, without the infernal swindles and capering of so much of contemporary cuisine, barbecue is truth; it is history and home, and the only thing I don't believe is that I'll ever get enough.

Jason Sheehan is a James Beard Award–winning restaurant critic for Denver's Westword *newspaper. His barbecue obsession began at age sixteen with a trip to Hercules Chicken and Ribs in his hometown of Rochester, New York. Although he worked as a chef for thirteen years, he lets his wife do the cooking at home.*

The People Have Spoken

Mark Shields

I BELIEVE IN POLITICS. In addition to being great fun, politics is basically the peaceable resolution of conflict among legitimate competing interests.

In a continental nation as big and brawling and diverse as ours, I don't know how else—except through politics—we can resolve our differences and live together. Compromise is the best alternative to brute muscle or money or raw numbers. Compromises that are both wise and just are crafted through the dedication, the skill, and, yes, the intelligence of our elected politicians.

I like people who run for public office. For most of us, life is a series of quiet successes or setbacks. If you get the Big Promotion, the hometown paper announces your success. It doesn't add, "Shields was passed over because of unanswered questions about his expense account" or "his erratic behavior at the company picnic."

But elections have been rightly described as a One-Day Sale. If you're a candidate, your fate is front-page news. By eight o'clock on a Tuesday night, you will experience the ecstasy of victory or you will endure the agony of defeat. Everybody you ever sat next to in study hall, double-dated with, or babysat for knows whether you won or, much more likely, lost. Politicians boldly risk public rejection of the kind that the rest of us will go to any lengths to avoid.

Having worked on four losing presidential campaigns earlier in my life and having covered the last seven as a journalist, I admire enormously the candidate able to face defeat with humor and grace. Nobody ever conceded defeat better than Dick Tuck, who upon losing a California state senate primary, said simply, "The people have spoken . . . the bastards."

But I believe in politicians who are courageous. The first time I ever slept in the same quarters with African-Americans or took orders from African-Americans was at

Parris Island in Marine Corps boot camp, and it was the political courage of one man, President Harry Truman, who ended the racial segregation of the U.S. military because he believed that fairness is at the heart of our values as a nation.

I admired the courage, too, of Ronald Reagan. In 1978, after voter initiatives discriminating against gays had prevailed in Miami, St. Paul, and Eugene, Oregon, a conservative-backed ballot measure in California to ban homosexuals from teaching in the public schools was favored to win until Ronald Reagan made the difference by campaigning—successfully—against it. Ronald Reagan opposed such intolerance in our public life.

I believe in the politics that wrote the GI Bill, that passed the Marshall Plan to rebuild a war-devastated Europe, that saved the Great Lakes, and that through Social Security took want and terror out of old age. The kind of politics that teaches us all we owe to those who came before and those who will come after. That each of us has drunk from wells we did not dig; that each of us has been warmed by fires we did not build.

At their worst, politicians (like the rest of us) can be petty, venal, and self-centered. But I believe politics, at its best, can help to make ours a world where the powerful are more just and the poor are more secure.

Mark Shields

> Mark Shields *has lived in and around politics for more than forty years. He started as an assistant to Wisconsin Senator William Proxmire, then worked on four presidential campaigns as well as numerous gubernatorial and congressional races. Shields is a political analyst for the* News-Hour *on PBS.*

Everything Potent Is Dangerous

WALLACE STEGNER,
AS FEATURED IN THE 1950S SERIES

IT IS TERRIBLY DIFFICULT TO SAY HONESTLY, without posing or faking, what one truly and fundamentally believes. Reticence or an itch to make public confession may distort or dramatize what is really there to be said, and public expressions of belief are so closely associated with inspirational activity, and in fact so often stem from someone's desire to buck up the downhearted and raise the general morale, that belief becomes an evangelical matter.

In all honesty, what I believe is neither inspirational nor evangelical. Passionate faith I am suspicious of because it hangs witches and burns heretics, and generally I am more in sympathy with the witches and heretics than with the sectarians who hang and burn them. I fear immoderate zeal, Christian, Moslem, Communist, or whatever, because it restricts the range of human understanding and the wise reconciliation of human differences, and creates an orthodoxy with a sword in its hand.

I cannot say that I am even a sound Christian, though the code of conduct to which I subscribe was preached more eloquently by Jesus Christ than by any other. About God I simply do not know; I don't think I can know.

However far I have missed achieving it, I know that moderation is one of the virtues I most believe in. But I believe as well in a whole catalogue of Christian and classical virtues: in kindness and generosity, in steadfastness and courage, and much else. I believe further that good depends not on things but on the use we make of things. Everything potent, from human love to atomic energy, is dangerous; it produces ill about as readily as good; it becomes good only through the control, the discipline, the wisdom with which we use it. Much of this control is social, a thing which laws and institutions and uniforms enforce, but much of it must be personal, and I do not see how we can evade the obligation to take full responsibility for what we individually do.

Our reward for self-control and the acceptance of private responsibility is not necessarily money or power. Self-respect and the respect of others are quite enough.

All this is to say that I believe in conscience, not as something implanted by divine act, but as something learned from infancy, from the tradition and society which has bred us. The outward forms of virtue will vary greatly from nation to nation; a Chinese scholar of the old school, or an Indian raised on the *Vedas* and the *Bhagavad Gita*, has a conscience that will differ from mine. But in the essential outlines of what constitutes human decency, we vary amazingly little. The Chinese and the Indian know as well as I do what kindness is, what generosity is, what fortitude is. They can define justice quite as accurately. It is only when they and I are blinded by tribal and denominational narrowness that we insist upon our differences and can recognize goodness only in the robes of our own crowd.

Man is a great enough creature and a great enough enigma to deserve both our pride and our compassion, and engage our fullest sense of mystery. I shall certainly never do as much with my life as I want to, and I shall sometimes fail miserably to live up to my conscience, whose word I do not distrust even when I can't obey it. But I am terribly glad to be alive; and when I have wit enough to think about it, terribly proud to be a man and an American, with all the rights and privileges that those words connote; and most of all I am humble before the responsibilities that are also mine. For no right comes without a responsibility, and being born luckier than most of the world's millions, I am also born more obligated.

> *Writer and educator* WALLACE STEGNER *published over thirty novels, collections of short stories and essays, and historical works.* The Big Rock Candy Mountain *was among his most popular novels, and* Angle of Repose *won the 1972 Pulitzer Prize for Fiction. Stegner wrote about the American West, and he also fought to protect it.*

A Balance between Nature and Nurture

Gloria Steinem

Is it Nature or is it Nurture? Heredity or Society? In that great debate of our time, conservatives lean toward the former and liberals toward the latter. But I believe both are asking the wrong question. I believe it's both nature and nurture and this is why:

I didn't go to school until I was twelve or so. My parents thought that traveling in a house trailer was as enlightening as sitting in a classroom, so I escaped being taught some of the typical lessons of my generation—for instance: that this country was "discovered" when the first white man set foot on it, that boys and girls were practically different species, and that Europe deserved more textbook space than Africa and Asia combined.

Instead, I grew up seeing with my own eyes, following my curiosity, falling in love with books, and growing up mostly around grown-ups—which, except for the books, was the way kids were raised for most of human history.

Needless to say, school hit me like a ton of bricks. I wasn't prepared for gender obsessions, race and class complexities, or the new-to-me idea that war and male leadership were part of human nature. Soon, I gave in and became an adolescent hoping for approval and trying to conform; it was a stage that lasted through college.

I owe the beginnings of rebirth to living in India for a couple of years, where I fell in with a group of Gandhians, and then I came home to the Kennedys, the civil rights movement, and protests against the war in Vietnam.

But most women, me included, stayed in our traditional places until we began to gather, listen to each other's stories, and learn from shared experience. Soon, a national and international feminist movement was challenging the idea that what happened to men was political but what happened to women was cultural; that the first could be changed but the second could not.

I had the feeling of coming home, of awakening from an inauthentic life. It wasn't as if I thought my self-authority was *more* important than external authority, but it wasn't *less* important, either. We are both communal *and* uniquely ourselves, not *either/or*.

Since then, I've spent decades listening to kids before and after social roles hit. Faced with some inequality, the younger ones say, "It's not *fair!*" It's as if there were some primordial expectation of empathy and cooperation that helps the species survive. But by the time kids are teenagers, social pressures have either nourished or starved this expectation. I suspect that their natural cry for fairness—or any whisper of it that survives—is the root from which all social justice movements grow.

So I no longer believe the conservative message that children are naturally selfish and destructive creatures who need civilizing by hierarchies or painful controls. On the contrary, I believe that hierarchy and painful controls create destructive people.

And I no longer believe the liberal message that children are blank slates on which society can write anything. On the contrary, I believe a unique core self is born into every human being; the result of millennia of environment and heredity combined in an unpredictable way that could never happen before or again.

The real answer is a balance *between* nature and nurture. What would happen if we listened to children as much as we talked to them? Or what would happen if even one generation were raised with respect and without violence?

I believe we have no idea what might be possible on this "Space Ship Earth."

GLORIA STEINEM *is a journalist and social activist in the feminist, peace, and civil rights movements. A fellowship to India in the late 1950s inspired her to fight for the rights of women and the poor. Steinem founded* Ms. *magazine in 1972 and is the author of four books.*

Life, Liberty, and the Pursuit of Happiness

Andrew Sullivan

I BELIEVE IN LIFE. I believe in treasuring it as a mystery that will never be fully understood, as a sanctity that should never be destroyed, as an invitation to experience now what can only be remembered tomorrow. I believe in its indivisibility, in the intimate connection between the newest bud of spring and the flicker in the eye of a patient near death, between the athlete in his prime and the quadriplegic vet, between the fetus in the womb and the mother who bears another life in her own body.

I believe in liberty. I believe that within every soul lies the capacity to reach for its own good, that within every physical body there endures an unalienable right to be free from coercion. I believe in a system of government that places that liberty at the center of its concerns, that enforces the law solely to protect that freedom, that sides with the individual against the claims of family and tribe and church and nation, that sees innocence before guilt and dignity before stigma. I believe in the right to own property, to maintain it against the benign suffocation of a government that would tax more and more of it away. I believe in freedom of speech, the right to offend and blaspheme, as well as the right to convert and bear witness. I believe that these freedoms are connected—the freedom of the fundamentalist and the atheist, the female and the male, the black and the Asian, the gay and the straight.

I believe in the pursuit of happiness. Not its attainment, nor its final definition, but its pursuit. I believe in the journey, not the arrival; in conversation, not monologues; in multiple questions rather than any single answer. I believe in the struggle to remake ourselves and challenge each other in the spirit of eternal forgiveness, in the awareness that none of us knows for sure what happiness truly is, but each of us knows the imperative to keep searching. I believe in the possibility of surprising joy, of serenity through pain, of homecoming through exile.

And I believe in a country that enshrines each of these

three things, a country that offers nothing but the promise of being more fully human, and never guarantees its success. In that constant failure to arrive—implied at the very beginning—lies the possibility of a permanently fresh start, an old newness, a way of revitalizing ourselves and our civilization in ways few foresaw and one day many will forget. But the point is now. And the place is America.

ANDREW SULLIVAN *was born in England and educated at Oxford and Harvard. At twenty-seven, he became editor of* The New Republic, *a position he held for five years. As a writer, commentator, and blogger, Sullivan addresses political and social issues and advocates for gay rights.*

Always Go to the Funeral

Deirdre Sullivan

I BELIEVE IN ALWAYS GOING TO THE FUNERAL. My father taught me that.

The first time he said it directly to me, I was sixteen and trying to get out of going to calling hours for Miss Emerson, my old fifth-grade math teacher. I did not want to go. My father was unequivocal. "Dee," he said, "you're going. Always go to the funeral. Do it for the family."

So my dad waited outside while I went in. It was worse than I thought it would be: I was the only kid there. When the condolence line deposited me in front of Miss Emerson's shell-shocked parents, I stammered out, "Sorry about all this," and stalked away. But, for that deeply weird expression of sympathy delivered twenty years ago, Miss Emerson's mother still remembers my name and always says hello with tearing eyes.

That was the first time I went unchaperoned, but my parents had been taking us kids to funerals and calling hours as a matter of course for years. By the time I was sixteen, I had been to five or six funerals. I remember two things from the funeral circuit: bottomless dishes of free mints, and my father saying on the ride home, "You can't come in without going out, kids. Always go to the funeral."

Sounds simple—when someone dies, get in your car and go to calling hours or the funeral. That, I can do. But I think a personal philosophy of going to funerals means more than that.

"Always go to the funeral" means that I have to do the right thing when I really, really don't feel like it. I have to remind myself of it when I could make some small gesture, but I don't really have to and I definitely don't want to. I'm talking about those things that represent only inconvenience to me, but the world to the other guy. You know, the painfully underattended birthday party. The hospital visit during happy hour. The shiva call for one of my ex's uncles. In my humdrum life, the daily battle hasn't been good versus evil. It's hardly so epic. Most days, my real battle is doing good versus doing nothing.

In going to funerals, I've come to believe that while I wait to make a grand heroic gesture, I should just stick to the small inconveniences that let me share in life's inevitable, occasional calamity.

On a cold April night three years ago, my father died a quiet death from cancer. His funeral was on a Wednesday, middle of the workweek. I had been numb for days when, for some reason, during the funeral, I turned and looked back at the folks in the church. The memory of it still takes my breath away. The most human, powerful, and humbling thing I've ever seen was a church at 3:00 on a Wednesday full of inconvenienced people who believe in going to the funeral.

DEIRDRE SULLIVAN *grew up in Syracuse, New York, and traveled the world working odd jobs before attending law school at Northwestern University. She is now a freelance attorney living in Brooklyn. Sullivan says her father's greatest gift to her and her family was how he ushered them through the process of his death.*

Finding Prosperity by Feeding Monkeys

Harold Taw

I COULD SAY THAT I BELIEVE IN AMERICA because it rewarded my family's hard work to overcome poverty. I could say that I believe in holding on to rituals and traditions because they helped us flourish in a new country. But these concepts are more concretely expressed this way: I believe in feeding monkeys on my birthday—something I've done without fail for thirty-five years.

When I was born, a blind, Buddhist monk, living alone in the Burmese jungle, predicted that my birth would bring great prosperity to the family. To ensure this prosperity, I was to feed monkeys on my birthday.

While this sounds superstitious, the practice makes karmic sense. On a day normally given over to narcissism, I must consider my family and give nourishment to another living creature. The monk never meant for the ritual to be a burden. In the Burmese jungle, monkeys are as common as pigeons. He probably had to shoo them away from his sticky rice and mangoes. It was only in America that feeding monkeys meant violating the rules.

As a kid, I thought that was cool. I learned English through watching bad television shows, and I felt like Caine from *Kung Fu*, except I was the chosen warrior sent to defend my family. Dad and I would go to the zoo early in the morning, just the two of us. When the coast was clear, I would throw my contraband peanuts to the monkeys.

I never had to explain myself until my eighteenth birthday. It was the first year I didn't go with my father. I went with my friends and arrived ten minutes after the zoo gates closed.

"Please," I beseeched the zookeeper. "I feed monkeys for my family, not for me. Can't you make an exception?"

"Go find a pet store," she said.

If only it were so easy. That time, I got lucky. I found out that a high school classmate had trained the monkeys for the movie *Out of Africa*, so he allowed me to feed his monkey. I've had other close calls. Once, a man with a pet monkey suspected that my story was a ploy, and that I was an animal-rights activist out to liberate his monkey. Another time, a zoo told me that outsiders could not feed their monkeys without violating the zookeepers' collective bargaining agreement. In a pet store once, I managed to feed a marmoset being kept in a birdcage. Another time, I was asked to wear a biohazard suit to feed a laboratory monkey.

It's rarely easy and, yet, somehow I've found a way to feed a monkey every year since I was born.

Our family has prospered in America. I believe that I have ensured this prosperity by observing our family ritual and feeding monkeys on my birthday. Do I believe that literally? Maybe. But I have faith in our family, and I believe in honoring that faith in any way I can.

Trained as an attorney, HAROLD TAW *is taking a break from legal work to complete his first novel,* Adventures of the Karaoke King. *He and his wife live in Seattle, where Taw has special arrangements with a local zoo to feed their Goeldi's monkey on his birthday this year.*

I Agree with a Pagan

Arnold Toynbee,
as featured in the 1950s series

I BELIEVE THERE MAY BE SOME THINGS that some people may know for certain, but I also believe that these knowable things are not what matters most to any human being. A good mathematician may know the truth about numbers, and a good engineer may know how to make physical forces serve his purposes. But the engineer and the mathematician are human beings first—so for them, as well as for me, what matters most is not one's knowledge and skill, but one's relations with other people. We do not all have to be engineers or mathematicians, but we do all have to deal with other people. And these relations of ours with each other, which are the really important things in life, are also the really difficult things, because it is here that the question of right and wrong comes in.

I believe we have no certain knowledge of what is right and wrong; and even if we had, I believe we should find it just as hard as ever to do something that we knew for certain to be right in the teeth of our personal interests and inclinations. Actually, we have to make the best judgment we can about what is right, and then we have to bet on it by trying to make ourselves act on it, without being sure about it.

Since we can never be sure, we have to try to be charitable and open to persuasion that we may, after all, have been in the wrong, and at the same time we have to be resolute and energetic in what we do, in order to be effective. It is difficult enough to combine effectiveness with humility and charity in trying to do what is right, but it is still more difficult to try to do right at all, because this means fighting oneself.

Trying to do right does mean fighting oneself, because, by nature, each of us feels and behaves as if he were the center and the purpose of the universe. But I do feel sure that I am *not* that, and that, in behaving as if I were, I am going wrong. So one has to fight oneself all the time; and this means that suffering is not only inevitable, but is an indispensable part of a lifelong education, if only one can learn how to profit by it. I believe that everything worth winning does have its price in suffering, and I know, of course, where this belief of mine comes from. It comes from the accident of my having been born in a country where the local religion has been Christianity.

Another belief that I owe to Christianity is a conviction that love is what gives life its meaning and purpose, and that suffering is profitable when it is met in the course of following love's lead. But I can't honestly call myself a believing Christian in the traditional sense. To imagine that one's own church, civilization, nation, or family is the chosen people is, I believe, as wrong as it would be for me to imagine that I myself am God. I agree with Symmachus, the pagan philosopher who put the case for toleration to a victorious Christian church, and I will end by quoting his words: "The universe is too great a mystery for there to be only one single approach to it."

English historian and historical philosopher ARNOLD TOYNBEE *was professor of modern Greek and Byzantine history and served as a delegate to the Paris Peace Conferences in 1919 and 1946. He achieved his greatest fame for his monumental twelve-volume work,* A Study of History.

Testing the Limits of What I Know and Feel

John Updike

A PERSON BELIEVES VARIOUS THINGS at various times, even on the same day. At the age of seventy-three, I seem most instinctively to believe in the human value of creative writing, whether in the form of verse or fiction, as a mode of truth-telling, self-expression, and homage to the twin miracles of creation and consciousness. The special value of these indirect methods of communication—as opposed to the value of factual reporting and analysis—is one of precision. Oddly enough, the story or poem brings us closer to the actual texture and intricacy of experience.

In fiction, imaginary people become realer to us than any named celebrity glimpsed in a series of rumored events, whose causes and subtler ramifications must remain in the dark. An invented figure like Anna Karenina or Emma Bovary emerges fully into the light of understanding, which brings with it identification, sympathy, and pity. I find in my own writing that only fiction—and rarely, a poem—fully tests me to the limits of what I know and what I feel. In composing even such a frank and simple account as this profession of belief, I must fight against the sensation that I am simplifying and exploiting my own voice.

I also believe, instinctively, if not very cogently, in the American political experiment, which I take to be, at bottom, a matter of trusting the citizens to know their own minds and best interests. "To govern with the consent of the governed," this spells the ideal. And though the implementation will inevitably be approximate and debatable, and though totalitarianism or technocratic government can obtain some swift successes, in the end, only a democracy can enlist a people's energies on a sustained and renewable basis. To guarantee the individual maximum freedom within a social frame of minimal laws ensures—if not happiness—its hopeful pursuit.

Cosmically, I seem to be of two minds. The power

of materialist science to explain everything—from the behavior of the galaxies to that of molecules, atoms, and their submicroscopic components—seems to be inarguable and the principal glory of the modern mind. On the other hand, the reality of subjective sensations, desires and—may we even say—illusions, composes the basic substance of our existence, and religion alone, in its many forms, attempts to address, organize, and placate these. I believe, then, that religious faith will continue to be an essential part of being human, as it has been for me.

JOHN UPDIKE *won two Pulitzer Prizes for his series of novels chronicling the life and death of Harry "Rabbit" Angstrom. He is also a noted poet and essayist, as well as a critic of literature and fine art. Updike grew up in rural Pennsylvania and now lives in Massachusetts.*

How Do You Believe in a Mystery?

Loudon Wainwright III

Here's a question: How do you believe in a mystery, in something you don't understand and can't prove? When we're children we're encouraged to believe in some mysterious things that turn out to not necessarily be true at all, things like the Tooth Fairy, the Easter Bunny, or the Flag. Naturally we're disappointed after our illusions have been shattered but usually we get over it. Some of us, however, become skeptical, even cynical, after that.

I've been asked on many occasions how I write my songs. Often I'll glibly reply, "I sure don't wake up in the morning and sharpen pencils." Then I'll admit how lazy and lucky I am and how successful and downright great some of the more notorious pencil sharpeners have been—two of my heroes, Frank Loesser and Irving Berlin, being among them.

If I'm feeling expansive I'll bring up the mysterious aspect, the mere 5 to 10 percent that matters the most, what's commonly called the inspiration. That's the thing beyond the technique and the discipline, when the sharpening and the gnawing stop, and something, as they say, "comes to you." It's a bit like fishing, really. There's certainly luck involved, but maybe what you took for laziness was (and I'm going out on a limb here) a sort of divine relaxation.

When I write what I consider to be a good song, when I realize it's going to hang together, when I somehow manage to get it into the boat, so to speak, I invariably find myself looking upward and thanking something or even, dare I say it, Someone. If I'm alone, my heartfelt thank-you is often an audible one. I've been known to mutter a few words at the head of the table at Thanksgiving dinner, or hoarsely whisper an "amen" at a wedding, funeral, or Christmas pageant, but usually it is just embarrassed lip service. As a rule I don't give thanks at a dinner table or in a church pew. For me, it happens when I've been hunched over a guitar for a few hours.

I believe in the power of inspiration, in the mysterious gift of creation. Creation with a small "c," that is, creation as in one's work, hauling in the day's catch. When I write a song, I'm happy for a few days and it's not just because I've been reassured that I still have a job, though that's certainly part of it. Mostly I'm happy, I think, because I've experienced a real mystery. I haven't the slightest idea how it happened or where or from whom or what it came. I'd prefer not to know. In fact, I'd prefer not to talk about it anymore. It might scare the fish away.

Singer-songwriter and actor LOUDON WAINWRIGHT III *has recorded more than twenty albums and was nominated for two Grammy Awards in the 1980s. Wainwright was raised in Westchester, New York, but spent his early years in Beverly Hills, California.*

Creative Solutions to Life's Challenges

Frank X Walker

I BELIEVE THAT WHAT WE OFTEN CALL SURVIVAL SKILLS is simply creativity at work.

When I think about how my mother fed all seven of us, making us think that every day was a "different meal," I still appreciate how much a creative cook can do with a single potato.

And it wasn't just in the kitchen. She would flip her old Singer sewing machine upright, study pictures in books and magazines, then make ethnic versions of those same dolls and stuffed animals to sell at church fund-raisers. Without a TV in the house to distract us, we made the dolls come to life, filling the hollow fabric sleeves one fistful of cotton at a time.

My mother made her own clothes and all my sisters' prom and wedding dresses. I always knew when she was making something, because she'd be singing or humming. She sang all the way through her home correspondence courses in floral design and interior decorating. She made being creative as normal as breathing and encouraged our participation by telling us that "idle hands and minds are the devil's workshop."

I believe that happy children are those given the freedom to be expressive, to discover, to create their own "refrigerator door" masterpieces. I remember mixing tempera paints with powdered detergent and painting the Baskin-Robbins windows every Christmas season. Not for money, but for all the ice cream I could eat. And every time I saw people look up at the window and smile, I knew I was getting the best part of the deal.

I believe that the highest quality of life is full of art and creative expression and that all people deserve it. I believe in a broad definition of what art is and who artists are: Barbers, cooks, auto detailers, janitors, and gardeners have as much right to claims of artistry as designers, architects, painters, and sculptors. Every day, our streets and school buses become art galleries in the form of perfectly spiked hair, zigzagging cornrows, and dizzying shoelace artistry.

My first collection of art was a milk crate full of comic books. I survived the projects and my teenage years inspired by my favorite character, the Black Panther, who had only his mind and no super powers, and Luke Cage, the thick-skinned, inner-city "Hero for Hire." By the time my "bookish" reputation and thick glasses became a target for the neighborhood bullies, I responded by composing juvenile, but truly "heroic" rhyming couplets in my head.

Ever since high school, words have continued to serve as my first weapon of choice, and my salvation. Many of life's challenges need creative solutions. I believe creativity—in all its many forms—can change the way we think and operate. Celebrating the creativity around us helps maintain our sanity and keeps us happy.

FRANK X WALKER *is assistant professor of English at Eastern Kentucky University. He coined the word "Affrilachian" to describe African-Americans living in Appalachia, and he helped found a group of Affrilachian poets. Walker is the author of three collections of poetry and was awarded a prestigious Lannan Literary Fellowship in 2005.*

Goodness Doesn't Just Happen

Rebecca West,
as featured in the 1950s series

I BELIEVE IN LIBERTY. I feel it is necessary for the health of the world that every man shall be able to say and do what he wishes and what is within his power, for each human being has a unique contribution to make toward our understanding of life, because every man is himself unique. His physical and mental makeup is unique, and his circumstances are unique. So he must be able to tell us something which could not be learned from any other source.

I wish I believed this only when I am writing about politics, but I believe it also in my capacity as a woman with a family and friends. I don't find it makes life easy. For if you let a man say and do what he likes, there comes a point when he wants to say or do something which interferes with the liberty of someone else to say or do what he likes.

Therefore, it follows that I see as the main problem of my life, the balancing of competitive freedoms. This involves a series of very delicate calculations, and you can never stop making them. This principle has to be applied in personal relations, and everybody knows that the Ready Reckoner to use there is love; but it takes a lot of real talent to use love effectively. The principle has to be applied in social relations also, and there the Ready Reckoner is the Rule of Laws, political scientists call it; a sense of mutual obligations that have to be honored, and a legal system which can be trusted to step in when that sense fails.

When I was young, I understood neither the difficulty of love nor the importance of law. I grew up in a world of rebellion, and I was a rebel. I thought human beings were naturally good, and that their personal relations were bound to work out well, and that the law was a clumsy machine dealing harshly with people who would cease to offend as soon as we got rid of poverty. And we were all quite sure that human nature would soon be perfect.

Yes, I can remember that when I was something like eleven years old, a visitor to my mother's home who had been in Russia described how she had one day been caught in the middle of a pogrom, and had seen the Cossacks knouting the Jews in the street. And I remember listening and thinking, "Now I mustn't forget this. People will be interested to hear of this when I'm old, because of course all this sort of thing will have died out long before." You can imagine what a shock it's been to me and my generation now that that sort of thing has become common form in many parts of the world, and such a pogrom, though horrible indeed, seems a small thing compared to the horrors millions have suffered today.

Horrors which were inflicted by human beings like me. I realize now that what's good on this earth does not happen as a matter of course; it has to be created and maintained by the effort of love and by submission to the Rule of Law. But how are we to manage to love, being so given to cruelty? How do we preserve the law from being corrupted by our corruption, since it's a human institution?

As I grow older, I find more and more as a matter of actual experience that there is a God, and I know that religion offers a technique for getting in touch with Him, but I find that technique very difficult. I hope I am working a way to the truth through my writing, but I also know that I must write to the thought of God in my mind for it to have any value. It's not easy; indeed, it's much more difficult than being a rebel. But I remind myself that if I wanted life to be easy, I should have got born on a different universe.

> *Critic, journalist, feminist, and novelist* REBECCA WEST *is perhaps best known for her studies of the Nazi war crimes trials in Nuremberg, for which President Harry Truman called her "the world's best reporter." In 1959, Queen Elizabeth named West a Dame Commander of the British Empire, the female equivalent of an honorary knighthood.*

When Ordinary People Achieve Extraordinary Things

Jody Williams

I BELIEVE IT IS POSSIBLE FOR ORDINARY PEOPLE to achieve extraordinary things. For me, the difference between an "ordinary" and an "extraordinary" person is not the title that person might have, but what they do to make the world a better place for us all.

I have no idea why people choose to do what they do. When I was a kid I didn't know what I wanted to be when I grew up, but I did know what I didn't want to do. I didn't want to grow up, have 2.2 kids, get married, the whole white picket fence thing. And I certainly didn't think about being an activist. I didn't even really know what one was.

My older brother was born deaf. Growing up, I ended up defending him, and I often think that is what started me on my path to whatever it is I am today.

When I was approached with the idea of trying to create a landmine campaign, we were just three people in a small office in Washington, D.C., in late 1991. I certainly had more than a few ideas about how to begin a campaign, but what if nobody cared? What if nobody responded? But I knew the only way to answer those questions was to accept the challenge.

If I have any power as an individual, it's because I work with other individuals in countries all over the world. We are ordinary people: My friend Jemma, from Armenia; Paul, from Canada; Kosal, a landmine survivor from Cambodia; Haboubba, from Lebanon; Christian, from Norway; Diana, from Colombia; Margaret, another landmine survivor, from Uganda; and thousands more. We've all worked together to bring about extraordinary change. The landmine campaign is not just about landmines—it's about the power of individuals to work with governments in a different way.

I believe in both my right and my responsibility to work to create a world that doesn't glorify violence and war, but where we seek different solutions to our common problems. I believe that these days, daring to voice your opinion, daring to find out information from a variety of sources, can be an act of courage.

I know that holding such beliefs and speaking them publicly is not always easy or comfortable or popular, particularly in the post–9/11 world. But I believe that life isn't a popularity contest. I really don't care what people say about me—and believe me, they've said plenty. For me, it's about trying to do the right thing even when nobody else is looking.

I believe that worrying about the problems plaguing our planet without taking steps to confront them is absolutely irrelevant. The only thing that changes this world is taking action.

I believe that words are easy. I believe that truth is told in the actions we take. And I believe that if enough ordinary people back up our desire for a better world with action, we can, in fact, accomplish absolutely extraordinary things.

Jody Williams is the founding coordinator of the International Campaign to Ban Landmines, which was awarded the Nobel Peace Prize in 1997. Williams previously did humanitarian work for people in El Salvador, Honduras, and Nicaragua. Her interest in advocacy began with a leaflet on global activism handed to her outside a subway station.

Afterword

The History of *This I Believe:*
The Power of an Idea

Dan Gediman

It was March 2003. I was home sick with the flu. I had read everything on my bedside table and was hungry for something else. I found a book on my wife's bookshelf that I had somehow never seen before. It was called *This I Believe.* I was intrigued by the words on the spine: "Written for Edward R. Murrow."

At first glance, I thought a fifty-year-old book filled with "the living philosophies of one hundred men and women in all walks of life" might be dry and dated. But I was wrong. It was as timely as could be.

Murrow's introduction to the book read as though he were reporting on events of today. He spoke of a time when "dissent is often confused with subversion," and when a man's beliefs and actions were "subject to investigation." Those words could have just as well come from the editorial pages of 2003, when America was gearing up for war in Iraq to fight the terrorists "over there" so they wouldn't attack us "over here." In addition, the Patriot Act was a center of controversy, also eerily reminiscent of the McCarthy era.

I quickly became absorbed in the book. Not only was the content on these pages fascinating to me, but the *idea* behind the pages captivated me as well: that all of these writers had dug deeply inside themselves to discern what they truly believed—and then had the courage to share it with the world. I wanted to know all I could about this project and how it had come about.

After many months of research, I learned the story of *This I Believe*. It all started Easter Sunday, 1949. Margot Trevor Wheelock, wife of a successful Philadelphia advertising executive, had clipped from a church bulletin a statement by theologian Joseph Fort Newton on the need for an inner balance to maintain one's life. When Mrs. Wheelock died the following week after a long illness, this clipping became very important to her husband, Ward Wheelock, triggering in him a need to examine his own beliefs, and to urge others to do so as well.

Shortly afterward, the idea of *This I Believe* was born at a business lunch attended by four powerful men: Ward Wheelock; William S. Paley, the founder and CEO of CBS; Donald Thornburgh, general manager of the local CBS affiliate in Philadelphia; and Edward R. Murrow, arguably the most famous—and most respected—broadcaster in the world at that time.

At this lunch, according to the recollections of Wheelock, the men bemoaned the spiritual state of the nation—that "material values were gaining and spiritual values were losing." They blamed a combination of factors, including "the uncertainty of the economic future, the shadow of war, the atom bomb, army service for one's self or loved ones, the frustration of young people facing the future."[1] To help counter this trend, the group decided to produce a daily five-minute radio program that would feature a well-known, successful man or woman sharing his or her personal philosophy—the guiding beliefs by which they led their lives. The hope was that these programs would be provocative, stimulating, and helpful to listeners.

---

[1] From a pamphlet entitled *This I Believe*, copyright 1951, Help Inc.

The plan was that Murrow would introduce each program and Wheelock would fund the series and act as its executive producer. Thornburgh would air it twice a day every weekday on his Philadelphia radio station. Paley would donate office space and studio time at his headquarters in New York, and if *This I Believe* were the success they hoped it would be, he would offer it to his entire network of CBS Radio affiliates.

Murrow and Wheelock, joined by veteran producer Edward P. Morgan, acted as the editorial board for the series, choosing whom to invite to participate. For their first batch of programs, they called on personal and professional contacts, choosing to begin with an eclectic mix of prominent people. The first twenty programs in the series included essays from a senator, several business leaders, a labor leader, two college presidents, a movie producer, a philosophy professor, a baseball umpire, and two certified national icons: Helen Keller and Eleanor Roosevelt.

Shortly after the start of the series, the *This I Believe* staff received a letter from a housewife who took them to task for only showcasing the prominent and prestigious. She was much more interested in hearing the beliefs of average citizens, such as herself. The editorial board took heed of her critique. Thereafter, the series took a decidedly more populist tack, featuring essays from cabdrivers, teachers, longshoremen, nurses, Pullman porters, incarcerated convicts, and, indeed, housewives. These were heard alongside an astonishing array of famous names, including ex-presidents Hoover and Truman, Supreme Court Justice William O. Douglas, popular actors such as Dick Powell and Barbara Stanwyck, sports figures such as baseball Hall of Famers Bobby Doerr and Jackie Robinson, literary giants such as Thomas Mann and Carl Sandburg, and a slew of Nobel laureates, including Albert Einstein.

When I interviewed former assistant producer Don Merwin about his involvement with *This I Believe*, he shared many illuminating stories. One of his tasks was to travel the country and oversee the recording of various essays. Sometimes that meant working with a local radio station, recording the essayist in the station's studios. Occasionally, it meant lugging a bulky tape recorder to the home or office of a prominent person. Merwin recalled taking the equipment to Albert Einstein's house in Princeton, New Jersey. "I started setting up, and Dr. Einstein, who was a very amiable man, was chatting with me and expressed curiosity about tape recording, which was fairly new in those days. He said, 'How does it work?' I started explaining the electronics of it, the way that the recording heads imprinted a signal on a moving tape. All of a sudden I froze up. I said, 'I'm lecturing to Albert Einstein on physics!'"

Merwin and his colleague Gladys Chang Hardy often worked closely with essayists on their scripts. Most people delivered an actual written essay, which then just needed some fine-tuning to be ready for recording. Some well-known people, however, lacked either the time or the ability to construct their own essay. A common remedy would be a trip to the library, where the *This I Believe* staff would do research and cobble together excerpts from the would-be essayist's published writings and arrange them artfully into a coherent script that the person would read into the microphone. Sometimes, Merwin and Hardy used even more heroic measures to capture an essayist's true beliefs.

Hardy recalled, "I talked to Martha Graham for four hours. She wanted to do the show but really didn't have time to put it together. So to put four hours of conversation into 600 words was a daunting task for me, which she, of course, edited and changed. But what was broadcast was [the beliefs of] Martha Graham."

Almost from the day the series first aired on Philadelphia's WCAU in March 1951, the response from the public was enormous and overwhelmingly positive. Indeed, before too long, Wheelock had assigned two secretaries at his agency the task of answering the daily mail. As the popularity of the series quickly spread, William Paley offered it to his network of CBS Radio affiliates. Some 196 stations around the country aired essays at least once daily during the week, sometimes two or more times on the weekend. In addition, *This I Believe* reached Americans through their daily newspapers as more than ninety papers throughout the nation published *This I Believe* pieces, usually as a weekly feature.

In 1952, the first of two volumes of *This I Believe* essays was published. It was an immediate success, selling out its first printing in a matter of days. It went on to sell over 300,000 copies in hardcover and was a Top-10 bestseller for three years. In addition, Columbia Records released a two-record set of *This I Believe* essays, which was also a best-seller.

The series quickly spilled over the U.S. borders and became an international phenomenon. The Voice of America translated *This I Believe* into six languages and broadcast the program daily throughout the world. In addition, the BBC signed on as a broadcasting partner, helping to choose and record over one hundred British essayists, which were then broadcast in both the United States and throughout the British Commonwealth. Due to the success of the British venture, another book was published, this time a volume containing the work of fifty American essayists and fifty British essayists. There was even an Arabic book, featuring a similar mix of American and Middle Eastern authors, which sold thirty thousand copies in Cairo in just three days.

Despite the increasing popularity of *This I Believe*, the series came to an abrupt end following two back-to-back blows to the Wheelock family. In early 1954, the Campbell's Soup Company pulled its business from Ward Wheelock's advertising agency. At the time, Campbell's accounted for about 90 percent of the agency's revenues. Without this income, Wheelock was no longer able to bankroll the radio series.

The final blow came in January 1955, when Wheelock, his new wife, and one of his two sons took a Caribbean cruise on his yacht. On January 18, 1955, the boat disappeared in the Bermuda Triangle. Wheelock's surviving son, Keith, remarked, "There has been nothing found since then. So that was not only the end of his life, but the end of any possible resuscitation of *This I Believe*."

In the wake of these events, Murrow agreed to pay out of his pocket the necessary expenses to finish production on a handful of remaining essays, and in April 1955, *This I Believe* distributed its last program to stations and slowly receded into obscurity.

Today, in the early twenty-first century, as my colleagues and I follow in the giant footsteps of Edward R. Murrow and his *This I Believe* staff, we are constantly reminded of the legacy we have inherited. We consider ourselves stewards of this powerful idea, not only in showcasing the beliefs of a new generation, but in allowing people to read the inspiring and still timely words of their parents' and grandparents' generation. After reading the archival essays contained in this book, I encourage you to visit our Web site at www.thisibelieve.org, and dig deeply into the treasure trove of other 1950s essays featured there. My hope is that you will be as amazed as I am at how eloquently these essays speak to us across the decades—and help us think about our own beliefs.

Appendix A

Introduction to the 1950s *This I Believe* Radio Series

Edward R. Murrow

This I Believe. By that name, we bring you a new series of radio broadcasts presenting the personal philosophies of thoughtful men and woman in all walks of life. In this brief time each night, a banker or a butcher, a painter or a social worker, people of all kinds who need have nothing more in common than integrity—a real honesty—will talk out loud about the rules they live by, the things they have found to be the basic values in their lives.

We hardly need to be reminded that we are living in an age of confusion. A lot of us have traded in our beliefs for bitterness and cynicism, or for a heavy package of despair, or even a quivering portion of hysteria. Opinions can be picked up cheap in the marketplace, while such commodities as courage and fortitude and faith are in alarmingly short supply.

Around us all—now high like a distant thunderhead, now close upon us with the wet choking intimacy of a London fog—there is an enveloping cloud of fear. There is a physical fear, the kind that drives some of us to flee our homes and burrow into the ground in the bottom of a Montana valley like prairie dogs to try to escape, if only for a little while, the sound and the fury of the A-bombs or the hell bombs or whatever may be coming. There is a mental fear, which provokes others of us to see the images of witches in a neighbor's yard and stampedes us to burn down his house. And there is a creeping fear of doubt—doubt of what we have been taught, of the validity of so many things we have long since taken for granted to be durable and unchanging.

It has become more difficult than ever to distinguish black from white, good from evil, right from wrong. What truths can a human being afford to furnish the cluttered nervous room of his mind with when he has no real idea how long a lease he has on the future. It is to try to meet the challenge of such questions that we have prepared these broadcasts. It has been a difficult task and a delicate one. Except for those who think in terms of pious platitudes or dogma or narrow prejudice—and those thoughts we aren't interested in—people don't speak their beliefs easily or publicly.

In a way, our project has been an invasion of privacy, like demanding a man to let a stranger read his mail. General Lucius Clay remarked, "It would hardly be less embarrassing for an individual to be forced to disrobe in public than to unveil his private philosophy." Mrs. Roosevelt hesitated a long time. "What can I possibly say that will be of any value to anybody else," she asked us. And a railway executive in Philadelphia argued at first that we might as well try to engrave the Lord's Prayer on the head of a pin, as to attempt to discuss anything thoughtfully in the space of five minutes.

We don't pretend to make this time a spiritual or psychological patent medicine chest where one can come and get a pill of wisdom to be swallowed like an aspirin, to banish the headaches of our time. This reporter's beliefs are in a state of flux. It would be easier to enumerate the items I do not believe in, than the other way around. And yet, in talking to people, in listening to them, I have come to realize that I don't have a monopoly on the world's problems; others have their share, often far, far bigger than mine. This has helped me to see my own problems in truer perspective. And in learning how others have faced their problems, this has given me fresh ideas about how to tackle mine.

Appendix B

How to Write Your Own *This I Believe* Essay

We invite you to contribute to this project by writing and submitting your own statement of personal belief. We understand how challenging this is—it requires intense self-examination, and many find it difficult to begin. To guide you through this process, we offer these suggestions.

Tell a story: Be specific. Take your belief out of the ether and ground it in the events of your life. Your story need not be heartwarming or gut-wrenching—it can even be funny—but it should be *real*. Consider moments when your belief was formed, tested, or changed. Make sure your story ties to the essence of your daily life philosophy and to the shaping of your beliefs.

Appendix B

Be brief: Your statement should be between 350 and 500 words. The shorter length forces you to focus on the belief that is central to your life.

Name your belief: If you can't name it in a sentence or two, your essay might not be about belief. Rather than writing a list, consider focusing on one core belief.

Be positive: Say what you do believe, not what you don't believe. Avoid statements of religious dogma, preaching, or editorializing.

Be personal: Make your essay about you; speak in the first person. Try reading your essay aloud to yourself several times, and each time edit it and simplify it until you find the words, tone, and story that truly echo your belief and the way you speak.

Please submit your completed essay to the *This I Believe* project by visiting the Web site, www.thisibelieve.org.

Appendix C

How to Use *This I Believe* in Your Community

One goal of this project is to facilitate a higher standard of active public discourse. We hope to inspire you to reflect, encourage you to share, and engage you in a conversation about personal values and beliefs that can shape your life, community, and our society.

And writing a *This I Believe* essay is just the first step.

We encourage you to come together with friends, neighbors, and acquaintances to discuss in a respectful manner the essays you've read or written—in the classroom, in public spaces, and in places of worship. To help you do this in your community, we offer these tools, which are available on our Web site, www.thisibelieve.org.

Appendix C

EDUCATIONAL CURRICULUM

This manual is designed to help teachers guide students in writing a *This I Believe* essay. Composed of several lessons, the curriculum is designed to help students understand the concept of belief and explore their own values by crafting a well-written essay. The guide includes sample *This I Believe* essays written by students as well as related exercises.

DISCUSSION GUIDES

We have produced a general discussion guide to help you engage a group in a moderated conversation about belief and values. It is appropriate for use in classrooms, civic clubs, libraries, senior centers, coffee shops, and other public venues. There is also a specifically tailored guide for use in houses of worship. Both guides include ground rules for structuring dialogue to ensure thought-provoking conversations, and tips for writing and sharing essays.

POSTER AND BROCHURE

We have designed print materials to help you spread the word about *This I Believe* activities happening in your community. Download a free poster or brochure that may be customized with specific details.

Acknowledgments

A project of this size requires much help along the way. Our team extends well beyond those on the title page of this book, but we begin there with our deepest thanks to John Gregory and Viki Merrick, who put their hearts into *This I Believe* from the beginning, and still do. Our editorial team of Bruce Auster, Emily Botein, Susan Feeney, and Ellen Silva, as well as our project photographer, Nubar Alexanian, have been invaluable. All of us have been guided by Edward R. Murrow and his team that preceded us in the 1950s, including Gladys Chang Hardy, Reny Hill, Donald J. Merwin, Edward P. Morgan, Raymond Swing, and Ward Wheelock.

Special thanks to Casey Murrow, Keith Wheelock, and Margot Wheelock Schlegel, the children of *This I Believe* foun-

Acknowledgments

ders Edward R. Murrow and Ward Wheelock, for their trust and counsel.

We are grateful to Studs Terkel, not only for his eloquent Foreword to this book, but for his leadership in the realm of listening.

This I Believe, Inc., is based in Louisville, Kentucky, and our crew there worked for years to bring this series back to the air. Great thanks to Amy Fisher, Jeff Gillenwater, Kathleen Hoye, Brigid Kaelin, MJ Kinman, and Joanna Richards. We are indebted particularly to Mary Jo Gediman for stepping in to offer assistance in the birth of this book.

Our production partner is Atlantic Public Media, Inc., in Woods Hole, Massachusetts, where all the essay submissions are reviewed by a dedicated group of readers, including Samantha Brown, Sydney Lewis, Chelsea Merz, Melissa Robbins, Helen Woodward, and Sarah Yahm. We thank the Cape and Islands public radio stations WCAI, WNAN, and WZAI, and their parent station, WGBH, for providing a home for that team.

At NPR we are grateful first to Jay Kernis, who championed the idea of reviving this series and agreed that NPR was the most appropriate modern broadcaster to inherit a project from Edward R. Murrow.

At every level, we put our trust in the reputation of NPR News for honesty and public service. Many in the news division guided the series along the way, including Davar Ardalan, Christine Arrasmith, Bob Boilen, Melissa Block, Madeleine Brand, Alex Chadwick, Neal Conan, Bruce Drake, Vladimir Dubinsky, Peggy Girshman, Sue Goodwin, Robin Gradison, Liane Hansen, Jeremy

Acknowledgments

Hobson, Steve Inskeep, Bob Malesky, Bill Marimow, Ellen McDonnell, Maeve McGoren, Sarah Mobley, Renee Montagne, Michele Norris, Quinn O'Toole, Jeff Rogers, Nathan Santamaria, Setsuko Sato, Robert Siegel, Graham Smith, Christopher Turpin, and Van Williamson.

The comprehensive Web site for *This I Believe* was built by the staff at NPR Digital Media, and we are indebted to all who participated, including Michael Horn, Melody Kokoszka, Joe Matazzoni, Bryan Moffet, Christina Nunez, Robert Spier, Maria Thomas, and Michael Yoch.

NPR has also provided administrative support for our series—technical production, underwriting and promotion, station services, business development, and countless other ways—with strong guidance from Stacey Foxwell and Ken Stern. Our thanks go to Julia Bailey, Carlos Barrionuevo, Chad Campbell, Frank Casamento, Jacques Coughlin, Bill Craven, Michael Cullen, Scott Davis, Kitty Eisele, Alyne Ellis, Meghan Gallery, Micah Greenberg, Penny Hain, Barbara Hall, Neal Jackson, Jane Kelly, Kevin Klose, Vanessa Krabacher, Jenny Lawhorn, Denise Leary, Jeeun Lee, Joyce MacDonald, Kathie Miller, Jeff Nemic, Eric Nuzum, Meredith Olsen, Ben Rogot, Marty Ronish, Emmy Rubin, Barbara Sopato, Andi Sporkin, Blake Truitt, Derek Turner, David Umansky, John Verdi, Barbara Vierow, and Roger Wight.

Nothing in public radio happens without funders, and we are enormously grateful to ours. *This I Believe* received the first faithful leap of funding from the Corporation for Public Broadcasting. Our thanks go to the able staff of CPB's radio and grants divisions, including Jeff Breslow, Deborah Carr, Kathy Merritt, and Sean

Acknowledgments

Simplicio. Our first year of broadcast was generously underwritten by Farmers Insurance Group, and for our second year we are grateful to Capella University. The balance of our budget was provided by The Righteous Persons Foundation, The Edith and Herbert Lehman Foundation, and many individuals who believed in this powerful idea, including Nolen Allen, Mr. and Mrs. Barry Bingham, Jr., Cornelia and Edward Bonnie, Christy and Owsley Brown II, the Reverend Georgine Buckwalter, Jill and Bill Cooper, Lois Cundiff, Beverly Giammara, Maurice Heartfield, Rowland and Eleanor Bingham Miller, David and Ona Owen, Marilyn Quinn, Joan Riehm, the Reverend and Mrs. Alfred Shands, Henry Wallace, James and Jane Welch, Mr. and Mrs. George Wheeler, and Dr. and Mrs. Richard Wolf.

The Public Radio Exchange (prx.org) helped us create our archive and makes essays directly available to public radio stations around the country. For that work, we thank Joshua Barlow, John Barth, Jared Benedict, Jake Shapiro, and Steve Schultze.

The public radio system is strong because it is decentralized and local. We salute all the individual stations that comprise the system and provide services to their own communities. We are particularly grateful to those stations that helped pilot *This I Believe* before we premiered nationally and who are still building the series from the grassroots up, including Capital Public Radio in Sacramento, KTOO Juneau, KUOW Seattle, KUT Austin, Vermont Public Radio, WBEZ Chicago, WCAI/WNAN/WZAI on Cape Cod, WFPL Louisville, WGBH Boston, WUSF Tampa, and WUWF Pensacola.

The creation of this book was immeasurably aided by our

ACKNOWLEDGMENTS

agent, Lynn Nesbit, and her associates at Janklow & Nesbit, including Mort Janklow, Cullen Stanley, and particularly Bennett Ashley. We are fortunate to have had their able services.

Our publisher, Henry Holt and Company, has been supportive throughout, always proving their belief in the heart of the project. We owe our thanks to John Sterling for his careful guidance and good taste, and to our thorough and dedicated editor, Vanessa Mobley. Also at Holt and its sister company Audio Renaissance, we are grateful to Patrick Clark, Barbara Cohen, Denise Cronin, Flora Esterly, Lisa Fyfe, Margo Goody, Jeanne-Marie Hudson, Meryl Levavi, Claire McKinney, Emily Montjoy, David Patterson, Rita Quintas, Maggie Richards, Mary Beth Roche, and Laura Wilson.

For their advice and assistance, we acknowledge our This I Believe, Inc., Board of Directors, Charles Baxter, David Handmaker, Todd Lowe, Greg McCoy, and Leslie Stewart; and our Advisory Board, Mark Cebuski, Gladys Chang Hardy, the Reverend Dr. Trace Haythorn, Ron Jones, David Langstaff, Joseph McCormick, Don Merwin, Casey Murrow, Carolyn Naifeh, Richard Paul, Howard Rheingold, Marita Rivero, Bill Siemering, Keith Wheelock, Dottie Willis, and James Wind.

For their help in myriad ways, we are grateful to Robert DePue Brown, David Domine, Art Chimes, and Mike Grey at the Voice of America, John Cooke of the Western Territories Group, Norman Corwin, Geoff Cowen of the University of Southern California Annenberg School of Communication, Elizabeth Deutsch Earle, Chris Enander, Adam Fiore, Dave Goldin, Chuck Haddix and Wendy Sistrunk with the Marr Sound Archives at the University of Missouri–Kansas City, Marty Halperin, Pemberton

Acknowledgments

Hutchinson, Elizabeth Kramer, Cameron Lawrence, Jim Lichtman, John McDonough, Michael Melford, Kurt Nauck of Nauck's Vintage Records, Toni Steinhauer, Stites & Harbison, PLLC, and their attorneys Jeremy Ballard, Jennifer Kovalcik, and James Seiffert, Les Waffen at the U.S. National Archives, and Barbara West. Many thanks to Georg Brandl Egloff for his elegant theme music. In addition, we owe a debt of gratitude to Kyna Hamill and Anne Sauer at the Digital Collections and Archives of Tufts University, as well as the Albert Einstein Archives at the Jewish National & University Library of the Hebrew University of Jerusalem.

And, finally, we offer our humble thanks and admiration to the thousands of individuals who accepted the challenge of writing a personal statement of belief and were willing to share it with everyone.

— Jay Allison and Dan Gediman

About the Editors

JAY ALLISON, the host and curator of *This I Believe*, is an independent broadcast journalist. His work appears often on NPR's *All Things Considered* and *Morning Edition* and PRI's *This American Life*, and has earned him five Peabody Awards. His essays have appeared in the *New York Times Magazine* and other publications. He is cocreator of Transom.org, which gives people the tools to tell their own stories, and of the Public Radio Exchange (prx.org), which helps get those stories on the air. Allison is the founder of the public radio stations that serve Martha's Vineyard, Nantucket, and Cape Cod, where he lives.

DAN GEDIMAN is the executive producer of *This I Believe*. His work has been heard on *All Things Considered, Morning Edition, Fresh Air, Marketplace, Soundprint, Jazz Profiles,* and *This American Life*. During his twenty-year radio career, Gediman has won many of public broadcasting's most prestigious awards for programs such as "Breaking the Cycle: How Do We Stop Child Abuse," and "I Just Am Who We Are: A Portrait of Multiple Personality Disorder." He also worked with legendary radio playwright Norman Corwin to produce "13 by Corwin" and "50 Years after 14 August," which won the duPont-Columbia Award.

From the Editors

One of our goals with this project is to compile as complete an archive as possible of Edward R. Murrow's 1950s series. You may be able to help us complete this task. If you possess any materials relating to *This I Believe*, be they recordings, newspaper or magazine clippings, essays written by yourself or a family member (perhaps a school assignment that you have kept over the years), or correspondence with the *This I Believe* staff, we would love to have copies for our archive. Thank you in advance for your help.

This I Believe, Inc.
P.O. Box 5031
Louisville, KY 40255-0031
admin@thisibelieve.org

READING GROUP GUIDE

A READER'S GUIDE FOR

This I Believe®

THE PERSONAL PHILOSOPHIES
OF REMARKABLE
MEN AND WOMEN

EDITED BY

Jay Allison

AND

Dan Gediman

Discussion Questions

1. Studs Terkel's foreword raises the question of truth and how we discern it. What do the essays in *This I Believe* tell us about the way we go about deciding what is true and what should not be believed? Do you think there are any absolute truths that apply to everyone?

2. In two essays reflecting the toll of war, Newt Gingrich emphasizes the need for vigilance ("I believe that the world is inherently a very dangerous place"), while John McCain celebrates the power of the quiet hero

("The truth worth of a person is measured by how faithfully we serve a cause greater than our self-interest"). What is your approach to the tides of danger and victory, destruction and reconstruction that have shaped the world for a long as history has been recorded? Do you think the future can be more peaceful than the past?

3. Several of the essays describe discrimination, such as Phyllis Allen's recollections of growing up in a racially segregated town, and Eve Ensler's observations about atrocities committed against women. What do you believe is at the root of discriminatory behavior? What causes some members of society to feel justified in causing the suffering of entire populations? How can we ensure equality in the face of the forces behind discrimination?

4. What did you observe about the essays from half a century ago compared with contemporary ones? Which issues have remained constant? What new ones have arisen that Edward R. Murrow's generation could not have imagined?

5. Questions of mortality and immortality are raised throughout the book, from Isabel Allende's response to her daughter's death to Elvia Bautista's experience of visiting her brother's grave. At the heart of many of these essays is the notion that love endures beyond a person's lifetime. How does this book define a life well-lived and a grief that is not in vain?

6. Martha Graham's "An Athlete of God" closes by describing the acrobat as "practicing living at that instant of danger. He does not choose to fall." In what way does this describe the tandem of fear and faith experienced in our daily lives? What does it take to "choose" not to fall?

7. What is the role of art and whimsy in shaping our beliefs? What do the contributors' words about fashion, reading, jazz, and other creative ventures say about the significance or value of imagination?

8. In "Seeing Beautiful, Precise Pictures," Temple Grandin describes how her ability to visualize resulted in humane new procedures for numerous livestock-handling facilities. What ethical balance shapes her

work? What small vision could you translate into grand action in your community?

9. The contributors to this book express a broad variety of viewpoints about religious beliefs, including the belief that there is no God (Penn Jillette) and the belief that we should protect our fellow human beings from harm, even when their religious affiliations are quite different from ours (Eboo Patel). What cultural observations are made in the essays on religion? What is its role in shaping identities and worldviews?

10. Benjamin Carson plays eloquent tribute to his mother in "There Is No Job More Important than Parenting." What qualities make her a good parent? What beliefs enabled her to sustain and inspire her son? Who has held a similar role of redemption in your life?

11. In what ways does *This I Believe* serve as a time capsule for the dawn of a new millennium? What conclusions will future readers draw about our era when reading these entries in another half century?

12. Which of the essays resonated with you the most? Did any of them inspire you to become an agent for change, either globally or simply in the way you affect the life of another individual?

13. What do you believe? What were your greatest influences in shaping those beliefs? How have your beliefs changed throughout your life?